DEMOCRACY AND THE ATHENIANS

MAJOR ISSUES IN HISTORY

Editor

C. WARREN HOLLISTER,
University of California, Santa Barbara

C. Warren Hollister: *The Twelfth-Century Renaissance*

William F. Church: *The Impact of Absolutism in France: National Experience under Richelieu, Mazarin, and Louis XIV*

C. Warren Hollister: *The Impact of the Norman Conquest*

Roger L. Williams: *The Commune of Paris, 1871*

L. Pearce Williams: *Relativity Theory: Its Origins and Impact on Modern Thought*

Loy Bilderback: *Conciliarism*

Robert O. Collins: *The Partition of Africa: Illusion or Necessity*

J. B. Conacher: *The Emergence of Parliamentary Democracy in Britain in the 19th Century*

Frank J. Frost: *Democracy and the Athenians*

Paul Hauben: *The Spanish Inquisition*

Bennett D. Hill: *Church and State in the Middle Ages*

Boyd H. Hill: *The Rise of the First Reich: Germany in the Tenth Century*

Thomas M. Jones: *The Becket Controversy*

Tom B. Jones: *The Sumerian Question*

Anthony Molho: *Social and Economic Foundations of the Italian Renaissance*

E. W. Monter: *European Witchcraft*

Donald Queller: *The Latin Conquest of Constantinople*

Jeffrey Russell: *Medieval Religions Dissent*

Arthur J. Slavin: *Humanism, Reform, and Reformation*

W. Warren Wagar: *The Idea of Progress Since the Renaissance*

DEMOCRACY
AND THE
ATHENIANS
Aspects of Ancient Politics

EDITED BY

Frank J. Frost

Professor of Ancient History
University of California, Santa Barbara

27426

John Wiley & Sons, Inc.
New York   London   Sydney   Toronto

Library of Congress Catalog Card Number: 70-81338
SBN 471 28340 1 (cloth)
SBN 471 28341 X (paper)

1 2 3 4 5 6 7 8 9 10

Printed in the United States of America

SERIES PREFACE

The reading program in a history survey course traditionally has consisted of a large two-volume textbook and, perhaps, a book of readings. This simple reading program requires few decisions and little imagination on the instructor's part, and tends to encourage in the student the virtue of careful memorization. Such programs are by no means things of the past, but they certainly do not represent the wave of the future.

The reading program in survey courses at many colleges and universities today is far more complex. At the risk of over-simplification, and allowing for many exceptions and overlaps, it can be divided into four categories: (1) textbook, (2) original source readings, (3) specialized historical essays and interpretive studies, and (4) historical problems.

After obtaining an overview of the course subject matter (textbook), sampling the original sources, and being exposed to selective examples of excellent modern historical writing (historical essays), the student can turn to the crucial task of weighing various possible interpretations of major historical issues. It is at this point that memory gives way to creative critical thought. The "problems approach," in other words, is the intellectual climax of a thoughtfully conceived reading program and is, indeed, the most characteristic of all approaches to historical pedagogy among the newer generation of college and university teachers.

The historical problems books currently available are many and varied. Why add to this information explosion? Because the Wiley Major Issues Series constitutes an endeavor to produce something new that will respond to pedagogical needs thus far unmet. First, it is a series of individual volumes—one per problem. Many good teachers would much prefer to select their own historical issues rather than be tied to an inflexible sequence of issues imposed by a publisher and bound together between two covers. Second, the Wiley Major Issues Series is based on the idea of approaching the significant problems of history through a deft interweaving of primary sources and secondary analysis, fused together by the skill of a scholar-editor. It is felt that the essence of a historical issue cannot be satisfactorily probed either by placing a body of undigested source materials into the hands of inexperienced students or by limiting these students to the controversial literature of modern scholars who debate the meaning of sources the student never sees. This series approaches historical problems by exposing students to both the finest historical thinking on the issue and some of the evidence on which this thinking is based. This synthetic approach should prove far more fruitful than either the raw-source approach or the exclusively second-hand approach, for it combines the advantages—and avoids the serious disadvantages—of both.

Finally, the editors of the individual volumes in the Major Issues Series have been chosen from among the ablest scholars in their fields. Rather than faceless referees, they are historians who know their issues from the inside and, in most instances, have themselves contributed significantly to the relevant scholarly literature. It has been the editorial policy of this series to permit the editor-scholars of the individual volumes the widest possible latitude both in formulating their topics and in organizing their materials. Their scholarly competence has been unquestioningly respected; they have been encouraged to approach the problems as they see fit. The titles and themes of the series volumes have been suggested in nearly every case by the scholar-editors themselves. The criteria have been (1) that the issue be of relevance to undergraduate lecture courses in history, and (2) that it be an issue which the scholar-editor knows thoroughly and in which he has done creative work. And, in general, the second criterion has been given precedence over the first. In short, the question "What are the significant historical issues today?" has been answered not by general editors or sales departments but by the scholar-teachers who are responsible for these volumes.

University of California,   *C. Warren Hollister*
Santa Barbara

CONTENTS

ATHENIAN POLITICAL DEVELOPMENT: A CHRONOLOGICAL TABLE
(ALL DATES B.C.)

620 The laws are first codified by Draco.

594 The constitution of Solon helps to correct legal, political, and economic abuses, and permits some expression of the popular will.

560-510 Constitutional government is suspended during the tyranny of Peisistratus and his sons.

508 Cleisthenes creates the constitution that endures for the next two centuries.

487 Archons are no longer elected but selected by lot. This greatly reduces the prestige of the higher magistracies.

480-479 Athens and the other Greek states repel the Persians.

476 Athens assumes leadership of the Delian League—a confederacy of Greek states allied against future Persian attack.

472-64 The first states attempt to withdraw from the Delian League but are forced into submission by Athens.

462 At the urging of Pericles and Ephialtes, the powers of the Areopagus are severely limited.

454 The treasury of the Delian League is moved to Athens, on the motion of Pericles.

450-49 Peace with Persia. Because the Delian League had been created as a defense against Persia, some states felt its usefulness had ended. Under the direction of Pericles, Athens maintains the League by force, thus changing it into an Athenian Empire.

444 Pericles' rival is ostracized. For the next consecutive fifteen years Pericles is elected general.

431 Outbreak of the Peloponnesian War.

429 Pericles dies during the plague. Cleon becomes the first commoner to dominate Athenian politics.

411 An oligarchic conspiracy seizes control for a few months.

405 End of the Peloponnesian War. Athens is forced to surrender to Sparta and a government of thirty "tyrants" is created and maintained in power by a Spartan garrison.

404-403 The democratic exiles return and lead a revolt against the tyranny. The old constitution is revived.

338 Athens is defeated by Philip of Macedon.

317 A local oligarch is made tyrant of Athens with the aid of Macedonian troops. End of the democratic constitution. From this time on, Athens is rarely free from foreign control, and participation in government is limited to persons of property.

DEMOCRACY AND THE ATHENIANS

INTRODUCTION: THE STRUCTURE
OF ATHENIAN POLITICS

Twenty-five centuries ago, the first successful direct democracy in the history of the world was created in Athens. By *direct* democracy, I mean that laws were made by the citizens themselves—no senators or deputies or councilors of any kind were allowed to dilute expression of the popular will. This much is clear.

But even today it is difficult enough to penetrate the semantic thicket surrounding the word "democracy." And democracy in antiquity is often said to be a meaningless term. Some critics, past and present, maintain that direct democracy is forever impossible: that it degenerates immediately into a mob-dominated anarchy. Others, wishing to appear realistic, agree with Pericles' mistress Aspasia that democracy is actually an aristocracy carried on with approval of the multitude.

This collection of readings provides a whole spectrum of opinion about Athenian democracy. Some arguments are reasoned and scholarly, others merely provocative; all will contribute to the continuing debate. Because most of the selections assume some prior knowledge of Athenian history and institutions, a few introductory remarks about the structure of the Athenian state may prove helpful.

It is not difficult to describe the mechanical operation of Athenian democracy. An Assembly of the People, which all male citizens might attend, met forty or more times a year and ruled on all policy, made laws, suggested and approved expenditures. *Ho Demos kratei*—the People rules—expresses the situation perfectly, and the abstract term *demokratia* was eventually coined to describe this sort of government.

A Council of Five Hundred was also chosen annually, but they were in no sense an Upper Chamber. The function of this body was administrative only; a rotating committee of the Council was in permanent session to take care of day-to-day business and to prepare the agenda for the Assembly.

In addition, a number of magistrates were chosen each year: archons, generals, financial officials, and so forth. But these men were allowed very little in the way of executive initiative or responsibility. Their duties were generally well defined, and at the end of their term of office any Athenian citizen might indict them for corrupt practices, favoritism, or simply incompetence. Therefore, it is not surprising that these men tended to think carefully before acting on their own, for the Athenian *Demos* was a jealous creature and ruthlessly punished those who sought to exceed their powers.

During the first half-century of the full democracy there also existed a Council of the Areopagus, created in the timeless past by the Goddess Athena herself, and containing all men who had once served as a higher magistrate. The Areopagus originally functioned as a sort of Supreme Court and evidently had a veto power over all other organs of government. But during the first three decades of the fifth century, this body gradually lost prestige until finally most of its powers were taken away and given to less exalted committees.

As can be seen in this brief sketch, the framework of Athenian government is disarmingly simple. All policy, all decisions, all law came from the Assembly of the People. All other bodies were administrative and designed simply to carry out the People's instructions. But the question inevitably arises: where in this system is there a place for the brilliant leadership of a Themistocles, a Pericles, or a Demosthenes? Statesmen like these gave Athens direction and made her famous. In what capacity did they operate?

The fact is that Athens' most notable leaders operated as private citizens, initiating policies by persuasive argument in the Assembly of the People. It is true that Pericles was a general for fifteen consecutive years, but this was exceptional in Athenian public life; at any rate, much of his program was enacted, despite strong opposition, before he was elected to the military post. And we hear much of the oppressive power of his successor Cleon, who manipulated Athenian policy for most of his career entirely as a private citizen. In fact, the first time he served as general the Athenian People forced him to do so against his will.

The Athenians referred to such an influential private citizen as *Prostates* of the *Demos*—roughly translated as "Leader of the People." His position depended on his popularity, his reputation for wisdom, and on general agreement among Athenians that he was worth listening to. His power resided in one single weapon: persuasion. The length of his term as unofficial advisor to the state rested entirely on the effectiveness of his advice. He might make his reputation with one single brilliant speech before the Assembly. One single recommendation that resulted in disaster could end his career in disgrace and obscurity—or even exile or death, for the Athenian Demos did not take bad counsel lightly. There might be times when two or even more men were generally conceded to be proper Leaders of the People. And there are, undoubtedly, periods when many spoke and many proposed but no one man possessed the charisma or the greatness of spirit to polarize the popular will around his person.

The changing fortunes of the Athenian state are linked to the personalities of these influential private citizens—not, as Aristotle thought, to changes of constitution or adjustments in the nature of the governmental institutions, all of which remained nearly the same for two hundred years. The nature of the Athenian state is mirrored in the persons whom the Athenian people trusted and to whom they turned for advice. When a problem was put to the Assembly and the herald asked, "Who wishes to speak?" the man, or men, on whom the people's gaze intuitively settled would accurately represent the direction the state was taking.

For the Athenian state was not a static collection of institutions, but a continually changing society of human beings. Even under the democratic constitution the Athenian Demos had not always ruled. Under the laws of Solon, a century before the lasting constitution was created, the people had been given *isonomia*—equality before the law and freedom from arbitrary arrest and punishment—but expression of the popular will was limited to a few meetings a year, or emergencies, when the people were invited to help the great men of the state in making decisions. Under the tyranny of Peisistratus and his sons, the people were treated well and, for the most part, according to the laws of Solon, but the popular assemblies met no more. Therefore, at the end of the sixth century, when a revolution led by aristocrats drove out the tyrants and created the constitution that was to endure, the people needed time to become accustomed to their new role. For one thing, the new laws reaffirmed the right of any man to stand up and address the Assembly. Understandably, the common man did not immediately take advantage of his new status, but was content for a time to let his imagined betters speak for him.

Despite the assertion of Aristotle (and after him, Marx) that there exists a permanent and irreconcilable hostility between nobles and commons, our evidence for Athens shows, beyond doubt, that reverence for the great princely houses of the aristocracy was intuitive and ingrained. These nobles, after all, could trace their ancestry back to a god. They were the only members of the state to have received a formal education. They were the men skilled in war who led the Athenian people out to great victories in 506, in 490 at Marathon, and in the Persian Wars of 480–479. Their deeds were sung by poets, their dedications crowded the temples, and their statues graced public places in Attica; paintings of their handsome young sons even adorned the lovely red-figured vases of the period.

It is not surprising, then, that the Athenian people were at first passive beneficiaries of the new constitution. But during the decades after the Persian Wars, they began to lose their awe for the gentry and to participate with more confidence in government.

The explanation of the change in their attitude is to be seen in the changing role of Athens as mistress of an empire that included over two hundred other city-states. The imperial responsibility that Athens quickly accepted after the defeat of Persia brought with it greatly expanded revenues and an enormous increase in the administrative arm of government.

Therefore, by creating a new class of wealthy men who were not gentlemen, the empire diluted aristocratic control of the economy, and by vastly increasing numbers of people in government service, it diluted aristocratic control of public business. For most of his lifetime, the aristocrat Pericles remained the people's choice, but in his later years he began to be challenged by commoners and after his death in 429 the Athenian Demos, for the first time, chose leaders from outside the ranks of the great aristocratic families. Never again were nobles to monopolize the leadership of the Athenian state.

But the Athenians never became egalitarian. They continued to require status of some kind in their statesmen, whether it was good family, wealth, military prowess or simply a reputation for moral probity. The great New England abolitionist Theodore Parker once said that Democracy meant not "I'm as good as you are," but "you're as good as I am." Rare as this sentiment may be in modern democracies, it is still less frequently encountered in ancient Athens. The mighty Pericles expressed it in his Funeral Oration, but didn't believe it; Socrates often said so, but only as a sly gambit to lead his opponent into demonstrating the reverse. From time to time, other Athenian writers or politicians gave lip service to the notion, but in actual fact, Athenians intuitively placed their confidence in men of achievement or property. When the comic poet Aristophanes, in 424, made fun of the politicians who were "in trade," or when Demosthenes, almost a century later, attacked his rival because his parents were of low caste and obscure origins, they were playing on what they knew were the sensibilities and prejudices of the Athenian public.

Even during the long summer of Athenian democracy, both the theory and the practice of popular government were undergoing ruthless examination. The philosopher Plato condemned the theoretical form out of hand: the People, when they are ruled by themselves instead of by their betters, become morally corrupt because they are motivated by their desires rather than by knowledge of what is best for them. Aristotle was preoccupied with organization and structure: "good" democracy was possible, he thought, but only if such a government possessed suitable institutions and constitutional safeguards to restrain the selfish impulses of the lower orders.

In the present day and age, we tend to be more pragmatic in our thinking about government. We hesitate to argue about theories as abstract as the evil effects of the popular will on man's search for virtue; the thoughtful person prefers to look behind paper institutions to see what is actually going on. Many countries, after all, have written constitutions that closely follow the model of the United States, but these documents only too often serve to mask sordid and corrupt despotism.

But the criticism of the great philosophers has had lasting influence. It is possible to show, after all, by manifold historical example, that democracies often do what is expedient rather than what is right—thus seeming to confirm Plato's suspicions. And a generation of European statesmen believed that the excesses of the French Revolution proved Aristotle's prediction of what the common people would do when unrestrained by law. Those who wish to show Athenian democracy heir to all those theoretical or structural weaknesses mordantly sketched by Plato and Aristotle have ample evidence.

In recent times, however, the pendulum has swung back toward an appreciation of the Athenian government and of the Athenian man in the street who made that government a success. For history also provides lessons, often of the nasty and painful sort, to show what happens in countries where expression of the popular will has been suppressed in the interests of efficiency, public order, and political philosophy.

1   Herodotus: A Constitutional Debate in Persia

The western coast of Asia Minor was rapidly colonized by Greeks from about the tenth century B.C. onward. Curiously, it is this frontier of the Greek world, generally referred to as Ionia, that saw the rise of that restless and inquiring spirit later held to be characteristic of all Greeks. Homer came from Ionia, as did the first lyric poets, and in following generations Ionia gave birth to philosophy,

SOURCE. From *Herodotus, The Histories* (III, 80–82) Aubrey de Sèlincourt, tr., Middlesex, England: Penguin Books Ltd., 1954. Copyright 1954. Reprinted by permission of Penguin Books Ltd.

science, and, as far as we know, the first written democratic con-
stitution, scratched onto a column of reddish stone on the island of
Chios sometime near the end of the seventh century. It is, there-
fore, not surprising that the first great historian of the Western
World was a product of the Ionian Enlightenment: the man whom
Cicero called the Father of History, Herodotus of Halicarnassus.

Born about 484 B.C., Herodotus was a small child during the
Persian Wars, but the consequences of this first World War were
still clear to all when, as a young man, he was forced into exile by
political disturbances in his hometown. After wide travels, which
impressed him with both the diversity and the universality of the
human animal, he settled at Athens, and it was perhaps here in this
city, now capital of an empire and rapidly becoming the intellectual
center of the Greek world as well, that he began to write his historie,
or "inquiry" into the Persian Wars. This masterful work traced the
causes of the conflict clear back to the Trojan War and beyond, with
long digressions on Babylonia, Egypt, and the other strange and
exotic societies on the periphery of the Greek world. But the main
theme was the rise of the Persian empire, its contacts and conflicts
with Ionia, and the seemingly inevitable involvement of the entire
Greek community.

Part of Herodotus' charm is his supposed naiveté—which may be
only a desire to preserve curious and droll stories for the entertain-
ment of his audience. If so, few of the historian's stories are as curious
as the following one, which dramatizes a debate among three Persian
nobles over constitutional forms; certainly no one else has ever
detected democratic tendencies among the Persian elite, nor, in fact,
have many people ever accused the Persians of having the slightest
interest in political science of any sort.

Nevertheless, Herodotus insisted that this debate took place, and so
it is reproduced here in its entirety. The scene is the Persian capital
at Susa, the time is about 521 B.C., and Darius and his fellow conspirators have just succeeded in toppling a usurper from the throne
in a palace coup.

Five days later, when the excitement had died down, the conspirators met to discuss the situation in detail. At the meeting certain speeches were made—some of our own countrymen refuse
to believe they were actually made at all; nevertheless—they were.
The first speaker was Otanes, and his theme was to recommend
the establishment in Persia of democratic government. "I think,"
he said, "that the time has passed for any one man amongst us to
have absolute power. Monarchy is neither pleasant nor good. You
know to what lengths the pride of power carried Cambyses, and
you have personal experience of the effect of the same thing in the
conduct of the Magus. How can one fit monarchy into any sound
system of ethics, when it allows a man to do whatever he likes
without any responsibility or control? Even the best of men
raised to such a position would be bound to change for the worse
—he could not possibly see things as he used to do. The typical
vices of a monarch are envy and pride; envy, because it is a natural
human weakness, and pride, because excessive wealth and power
lead to the delusion that he is something more than a man. These
two vices are the root cause of all wickedness: both lead to acts of
savage and unnatural violence. Absolute power ought, by rights,
to preclude envy on the principle that the man who possesses it
has also at command everything he could wish for; but in fact it
is not so, as the behaviour of kings to their subjects proves: they
are jealous of the best of them merely for continuing to live, and
take pleasure in the worst; and no one is readier than a king to
listen to tale-bearers. A king, again, is the most inconsistent of
men; show him reasonable respect, and he is angry because you do
not abase yourself before his majesty; abase yourself, and he hates
you for being a superserviceable rogue. But the worst of all
remains to be said—he breaks up the structure of ancient tradition
and law, forces women to serve his pleasure, and puts men to death
without trial. Contrast with this the rule of the people: first, it
has the finest of all names to describe it—*isonomy*, or equality
before the law; and, secondly, the people in power do none of the
things that monarchs do. Under a government of the people a
magistrate is appointed by lot and is held responsible for his conduct in office, and all questions are put up for open debate. For
these reasons I propose that we do away with the monarchy, and

raise the people to power; for the state and the people are synonymous terms."

Otanes was followed by Megabyzus, who recommended the principle of oligarchy in the following words: "In so far as Otanes spoke in favour of abolishing monarchy, I agree with him; but he is wrong in asking us to transfer political power to the people. The masses are a feckless lot—nowhere will you find more ignorance or irresponsibility or violence. It would be an intolerable thing to escape the murderous caprice of a king, only to be caught by the equally wanton brutality of the rabble. A king does at least act consciously and deliberately; but the mob does not. Indeed how should it, when it has never been taught what is right and proper, and has no knowledge of its own about such things? The masses have not a thought in their heads; all they can do is to rush blindly into politics and sweep all before them like a river in flood. As for the people, then, let them govern Persia's enemies, not Persia; and let us ourselves choose a certain number of the best men in the country, and give *them* political power. We personally shall be amongst them, and it is only natural to suppose that the best men will produce the best policy."

Darius was the third to speak. "I support," he said, "all Megabyzus' remarks about the masses, but I do not agree with what he said of oligarchy. Take the three forms of government we are considering—democracy, oligarchy, and monarchy—and suppose each of them to be the best of its kind; I maintain that the third is greatly preferable to the other two. One ruler: it is impossible to improve upon that—provided he is the best man for the job. His judgement will be in keeping with his character; his control of the people will be beyond reproach; his measures against enemies and traitors will be kept secret more easily than under other forms of government. In an oligarchy, the fact that a number of men are competing for distinction in the public service cannot but lead to violent personal feuds; each of them wants to get to the top, and to see his own proposals carried; so they quarrel. Personal quarrels lead to open dissension, and then to bloodshed; and from that state of affairs the only way out is a return to monarchy—a clear proof that monarchy is best. Again, in a democracy, malpractices are bound to occur; in this case, however, corrupt dealings in government services lead not to private feuds, but to close personal associations, the men responsible for them putting their heads together and mutually supporting one another. And so it goes on, until somebody or other comes forward as the people's champion and breaks up the cliques which are out for their own interests. This wins him the admiration of the mob, and as a result he soon finds himself entrusted with absolute power—all of which is another proof that the best form of government is monarchy. To sum up: where did we get our freedom from, and who gave it to us? Is it the result of democracy, or of oligarchy, or of monarchy? We were set free by one man, and therefore I propose that we should preserve that form of government, and, further, that we should refrain from changing ancient laws, which have served us well in the past. To do so would lead only to disaster."

2 The "Old Oligarch": A Gentleman Condemns Democracy

The Athenian aristocracy and commons worked together, for the most part, in harmony, with mutual respect, and without that class warfare that Aristotle and others believed ought to exist in all societies. But to some Athenians of the more privileged classes it must have seemed as if their old way of life, their old prerogatives, wealth, and influence had vanished, destroyed by the growing confidence and prosperity of what they regarded as the lower orders. Such a man is the author of the following tract.

The Constitution of the Athenians is a satirical picture of the Athenian democracy as the writer saw it in the days just before the Peloponnesian War: mob rule is supreme, the masses control all departments of government, vote themselves honors and entertainments, and rigorously exclude the "better" classes from public life.

Although this tract has come down to us in the manuscripts of the

SOURCE. From *The Greek Historians*, Volume II, Francis R. B. Godolphin, ed., New York: Random House, 1942, pp. 633–643. Copyright 1942 by Random House, Inc. Reprinted by permission of Random House, Inc.

later historian Xenophon, it is obviously not his work. The style is completely different and the historical content shows that it was written before Xenophon was born. Lacking a name, modern scholars have been content to call the author "The Old Oligarch," and he richly deserves the title. But despite the abuses he feels he and his class have been subjected to, his commentary is not without humor, nor does he fail to admire the efficiency with which the "worse" sort of people pursue their self interest.

---

1. Now, as for the constitution of the Athenians, and the type or manner of constitution which they have chosen, I praise it not, in so far as the very choice involves the welfare of the baser folk as opposed to that of the better class.[1] I repeat, I withhold my praise so far; but, given the fact that this is the type agreed upon, I propose to show that they set about its preservation in the right way; and that those other transactions in connection with it, which are looked upon as blunders by the rest of the Hellenic world, are the reverse.

In the first place, I maintain, it is only just that the poorer classes and the common people of Athens should be better off than the men of birth and wealth, seeing that it is the people who man the fleet, and have brought the city her power. The steersman, the boatswain, the lieutenant, the look-out-man at the prow, the ship-wright—these are the people who supply the city with power far rather than her heavy infantry and men of birth and quality. This being the case, it seems only just that offices of state should be thrown open to every one both in the ballot and the show of hands, and that the right of speech should belong to any one who likes, without restriction. For, observe, there are many of these offices which, according as they are in good or bad hands, are a source of safety or of danger to the People, and in these the People prudently abstains from sharing; as, for instance, it does not think it incumbent on itself to share in the functions of the

---

[1] It should be remembered throughout that the "better" citizens are the friends of the Old Oligarch and that the "worse" are democrats.

general or of the commander of cavalry. The commons recognises the fact that in forgoing the personal exercises of these offices, and leaving them to the control of the more powerful citizens, it secures the balance of advantage to itself. It is only those departments of government which bring pay and assist the private estate than the People cares to keep in its own hands.

In the next place, in regard to what some people are puzzled to explain—the fact that everywhere greater consideration is shown to the base, to poor people and to common folk, than to persons of good quality,—so far from being a matter of surprise, this, as can be shown, is the keystone of the preservation of the democracy. It is these poor people, this common folk, this worse element, whose prosperity, combined with the growth of their numbers, enhances the democracy. Whereas, a shifting of fortune to the advantage of the wealthy and the better classes implies the establishment on the part of the commons of a strong power in opposition to itself. In fact, all the world over, the cream of society is in opposition to the democracy. Naturally, since the smallest amount of intemperance and injustice, together with the highest scrupulousness in the pursuit of excellence, is to be found in the ranks of the better class, while within the ranks of the People will be found the greatest amount of ignorance, disorderliness, rascality,—poverty acting as a stronger incentive to base conduct, not to speak of lack of education and ignorance, traceable to the lack of means which afflicts the average of mankind.

The objection may be raised that it was a mistake to allow the universal right of speech and a seat in council. These should have been reserved for the cleverest, the flower of the community. But here, again, it will be found that they are acting with wise deliberation in granting to even the baser sort the right of speech, for supposing only the better people might speak, or sit in council, blessings would fall to the lot of those like themselves, but to the commons the reverse of blessings. Whereas now, any one who likes, any base fellow, may get up and discover something to the advantage of himself and his equals. It may be retorted, "And what sort of advantage either for himself or for the People can such a fellow be expected to hit upon?" The answer to which is, that in their judgment the ignorance and the baseness of this fellow, together with his goodwill, are worth a great deal more to them than your superior person's virtue and wisdom, coupled with animosity. What it comes to, therefore, is that a state founded upon such institutions will not be the best state; but, given a democracy, these are the right means to secure its preservation. The People, it must be borne in mind, does not demand that the city should be well governed and itself a slave. It desires to be free and to be master. As to bad legislation it does not concern itself about that. In fact, what you believe to be bad legislation is the very source of the People's strength and freedom. But if you seek for good legislation, in the first place you will see the cleverest members of the community laying down the laws for the rest. And in the next place, the better class will curb and chastise the lower orders; the better class will deliberate in behalf of the state, and not suffer crack-brained fellows to sit in council, or to speak or vote in the assemblies. No doubt; but under the weight of such blessings the People will in a very short time be reduced to slavery.

Another point is the extraordinary amount of license granted to slaves and resident aliens at Athens, where a blow is illegal, and a slave will not step aside to let you pass him in the street. I will explain the reason of this peculiar custom. Supposing it were legal for a slave to be beaten by a free citizen, or for a resident alien or freedman to be beaten by a citizen, it would frequently happen that an Athenian might be mistaken for a slave or an alien and receive a beating; since the Athenian People is not better clothed than the slave or alien, nor in personal appearance is there any superiority. Or if the fact itself that slaves in Athens are allowed to indulge in luxury, and indeed in some cases to live magnificently, be found astonishing, this too, it can be shown, is done of set purpose. Where you have a naval power dependent upon wealth we must perforce be slaves to our slaves, in order that we may get in our slave-rents, and let the real slave go free. Where you have wealthy slaves it ceases to be advantageous that my slave should stand in awe of you. In Lacedaemon my slave stands in awe of you. But if your slave is in awe of me there will be a risk of his giving away his own moneys to avoid running a risk in his own person. It is for this reason then that we have established an equality between our slaves and free men; and again between our resident aliens and full citizens, because the city stands in need of her resident aliens to meet the requirements of such a multiplicity of arts and for the purposes of her navy. That is, I repeat, the justification of the equality conferred upon our resident aliens.

The common people put a stop to citizens devoting their time to athletics and to the cultivation of music, disbelieving in the beauty of such training, and recognising the fact that these are things the cultivation of which is beyond its power. On the same principle, in the case of the choregia,[2] the management of athletics, and the command of ships, the fact is recognised that it is the rich man who trains the chorus, and the People for whom the chorus is trained; it is the rich man who is naval commander or superintendent of athletics, and the People that profits by their labours. In fact, what the People looks upon as its right is to pocket the money. To sing and run and dance and man the vessels is well enough, but only in order that the People may be the gainer, while the rich are made poorer. And so in the courts of justice, justice is not more an object of concern to the jurymen than what touches personal advantage.

To speak next of the allies, and in reference to the point that emissaries from Athens come out, and, according to common opinion, calumniate and vent their hatred upon the better sort of people, this is done on the principle that the ruler cannot help being hated by those whom he rules; but that if wealth and respectability are to wield power in the subject cities the empire of the Athenian People has but a short lease of existence. This explains why the better people are punished with infamy, robbed of their money, driven from their homes, and put to death, while the baser sort are promoted to honour. On the other hand, the better Athenians protect the better class in the allied cities. And why? Because they recognise that it is to the interest of their own class at all times to protect the best element in the cities. It may be urged that if it comes to strength and power the real strength of Athens lies in the capacity of her allies to contribute their money quota. But to

---

[2] The duties of the choregia consisted in finding maintenance and instruction for the dramatic chorus.

the democratic mind it appears a higher advantage still for the individual Athenian to get hold of the wealth of the allies, leaving them only enough to live upon and to cultivate their estates, but powerless to harbour treacherous designs.

Again, it is looked upon as a mistaken policy on the part of the Athenian democracy to compel her allies to voyage to Athens in order to have their cases tried. On the other hand, it is easy to reckon up what a number of advantages the Athenian People derives from the practice impugned. In the first place, there is the steady receipt of salaries throughout the year derived from the court fees. Next, it enables them to manage the affairs of the allied states while seated at home without the expense of naval expeditions. Thirdly, they thus preserve the partisans of the democracy, and ruin her opponents in the law courts. Whereas, supposing the several allied states tried their cases at home, being inspired by hostility to Athens, they would destroy those of their own citizens whose friendship to the Athenian People was most marked. But besides all this the democracy derives the following advantages from hearing the cases of her allies in Athens. In the first place, the one per cent[3] levied in Piraeus is increased to the profit of the state; again, the owner of a lodging-house does better, and so, too, the owner of a pair of beasts, or of slaves to be let out on hire; again, heralds and criers are a class of people who fare better owing to the sojourn of foreigners at Athens. Further still, supposing the allies had not to resort to Athens for the hearing of cases, only the official representative of the imperial state would be held in honour, such as the general, or trierarch, or ambassador. Whereas now every single individual among the allies is forced to pay flattery to the People of Athens because he knows that he must betake himself to Athens and win or lose his case at the bar, not of any stray set of judges, but of the sovereign People itself, such being the law and custom at Athens. He is compelled to behave as a suppliant in the courts of justice, and when some juryman comes into court, to grasp his hand. For this reason, therefore, the allies find themselves more and more in the position of slaves to the people of Athens.

[3] The text probably should read five per cent.

Furthermore, owing to the possession of property beyond the limits of Attica, and the exercise of magistracies which take them into regions beyond the frontier, they and their attendants have insensibly acquired the art of navigation. A man who is perpetually voyaging is forced to handle the oar, he and his domestic alike, and to learn the terms familiar in seamanship. Hence a stock of skilful mariners is produced, bred upon a wide experience of voyaging and practice. They have learned their business, some in piloting a small craft, others a merchant vessel, while others have been drafted off from these for service on a ship-of-war. So that the majority of them are able to row the moment they set foot on board a vessel, having been in a state of preliminary practice all their lives.

2. As to the heavy infantry, an arm the deficiency of which at Athens is well recognised, this is how the matter stands. They recognise the fact that, in reference to the hostile power, they are themselves inferior, and must be, even if their heavy infantry were more numerous. But relatively to the allies, who bring in the tribute, their strength even on land is enormous. And they are persuaded that their heavy infantry is sufficient for all purposes, provided they retain this superiority. Apart from all else, to a certain extent fortune must be held responsible for the actual condition. The subjects of a power which is dominant by land have it open to them to form contingents from several small states and to muster in force for battle. But with the subjects of a naval power it is different. As far as they are groups of islanders it is impossible for their states to meet together for united action, for the sea lies between them, and the dominant power is master of the sea. And even if it were possible for them to assemble in some single island unobserved, they would only do so to perish by famine. And as to the states subject to Athens which are not islanders, but situated on the continent, the larger are held in check by need and the small ones absolutely by fear, since there is no state in existence which does not depend upon imports and exports, and these she will forfeit if she does not lend a willing ear to those who are masters by sea. In the next place, a power dominant by sea can do certain things which a land power is debarred from doing; as, for instance, ravage the territory of a

superior, since it is always possible to coast along to some point, where either there is no hostile force to deal with or merely a small body; and in case of an advance in force on the part of the enemy they can take to their ships and sail away. Such a performance is attended with less difficulty than that experienced by the relieving force on land. Again, it is open to a power so dominating by sea to leave its own territory and sail off on as long a voyage as you please. Whereas the land power cannot place more than a few days' journey between itself and its own territory, for marches are slow affairs; and it is not possible for an army on the march to have food supplies to last for any great length of time. Such an army must either march through friendly territory or it must force a way by victory in battle. The voyager meanwhile has it in his power to disembark at any point where he finds himself in superior force, or, at the worst, to coast by until he reaches either a friendly district or an enemy too weak to resist. Again, those diseases to which the fruits of the earth are liable as visitations from heaven fall severely on a land power, but are scarcely felt by the naval power, for such sicknesses do not visit the whole earth everywhere at once. So that the ruler of the sea can get in supplies from a thriving district. And if one may descend to more trifling particulars, it is to this same lordship of the sea that the Athenians owe the discovery, in the first place, of many of the luxuries of life through intercourse with other countries. So that the choice things of Sicily and Italy, of Cyprus and Egypt and Lydia, of Pontus or Peloponnese, or wheresoever else it be, are all swept, as it were, into one centre, and all owing, as I say, to their maritime empire. And again, in process of listening to every form of speech, they have selected this from one place and that from another—for themselves. So much so that while the rest of the Hellenes employ each pretty much their own peculiar mode of speech, habit of life, and style of dress, the Athenians have adopted a composite type, to which all sections of Hellas, and the foreigner alike, have contributed.

As regards sacrifices and temples and festivals and sacred enclosures, the People sees that it is not possible for every poor citizen to do sacrifice and hold festival, or to set up temples and to inhabit a large and beautiful city. But it has hit upon a means of meeting the difficulty. They sacrifice—that is, the whole state sacrifices—at the public cost a large number of victims; but it is the People that keeps holiday and distributes the victims by lot among its members. Rich men have in some cases private gymnasia and baths with dressing-rooms, but the People takes care to have built at the public cost a number of palaestras, dressing-rooms, and bathing establishments for its own special use, and the mob gets the benefit of the majority of these, rather than the select few or the well-to-do.

As to wealth, the Athenians are exceptionally placed with regard to Hellenic and foreign communities alike, in their ability to hold it. For, given that some state or other is rich in timber for shipbuilding, where is it to find a market for the product except by persuading the ruler of the sea? Or, suppose the wealth of some state or other to consist of iron, or may be of bronze, or of linen yarn, where will it find a market except by permission of the supreme maritime power? Yet these are the very things, you see, which I need for my ships. Timber I must have from one, and from another iron, from a third bronze, from a fourth linen yarn, from a fifth wax. Besides which they will not suffer their antagonists in those parts to carry these products elsewhere, or they will cease to use the sea. Accordingly I, without one stroke of labour, extract from the land and possess all these good things, thanks to my supremacy on the sea; while not a single other state possesses the two of them. Not timber, for instance, and yarn together, the same city. But where yarn is abundant, the soil will be light and devoid of timber. And in the same way bronze and iron will not be products of the same city. And so for the rest, never two, or at best three, in one state, but one thing here and another thing there. Moreover, above and beyond what has been said, the coastline of every mainland presents, either some jutting promontory, or adjacent island, or narrow strait of some sort, so that those who are masters of the sea can come to moorings at one of these points and wreak vengeance on the inhabitants of the mainland.

There is just one thing which the Athenians lack. Supposing they were the inhabitants of an island, and were still, as now, rulers of the sea, they would have had it in their power to work whatever mischief they liked, and to suffer no evil in return (as long as they kept command of the sea), neither the ravaging of their territory nor the expectation of an enemy's approach. Whereas at present the farming portion of the community and the wealthy landowners are ready to cringe before the enemy overmuch, while the People, knowing full well that, come what may, not one stock or stone of their property will suffer, nothing will be cut down, nothing burnt, lives in freedom from alarm, without fawning at the enemy's approach. Besides this, there is another fear from which they would have been exempt in an island home—the apprehension of the city being at any time betrayed by their oligarchs and the gates thrown open, and an enemy bursting suddenly in. How could incidents like these have taken place if an island had been their home? Again, had they inhabited an island there would have been no stirring of sedition against the People; whereas at present, in the event of faction, those who set it on foot base their hopes of success on the introduction of an enemy by land. But a people inhabiting an island would be free from all anxiety on that score. Since, however, they did not chance to inhabit an island from the first, what they now do is this— they deposit their property in the islands, trusting to their command of the sea, and they suffer the soil of Attica to be ravaged without a sigh. To expend pity on that, they know, would be to deprive themselves of other blessings still more precious.

Further, states oligarchically governed are forced to ratify their alliances and solemn oaths, and if they fail to abide by their contracts, the offence, by whomsoever committed, lies nominally at the door of the oligarchs who entered upon the contract. But in the case of engagements entered into by a democracy it is open to the People to throw the blame on the single individual who spoke in favour of some measure, or put it to the vote, and to maintain to the rest of the world, "I was not present, nor do I approve of the terms of the agreement," Inquiries are made in a full meeting of the People, and should any of these things be disapproved of, they can at once discover countless excuses to avoid doing whatever they do not wish. And if any mischief should spring out of any resolutions which the People has passed in council, the People can readily shift the blame from its own shoulders. "A handful of oligarchs acting against the interests of the People have ruined us." But if any good result ensue, they, the People, at once take the credit of that to themselves.

In the same spirit it is not allowed to caricature on the comic stage or otherwise libel the People, because they do not care to hear themselves ill spoken of. But if any one has a desire to satirise his neighbour he has full leave to do so. And this because they are well aware that, as a general rule, the person caricatured does not belong to the People, or the masses. He is more likely to be some wealthy or well-born person, or man of means and influence. In fact, but few poor people and of the popular stamp incur the comic lash, or if they do they have brought it on themselves by excessive love of meddling or some covetous self-seeking at the expense of the People, so that no particular annoyance is felt at seeing such folk satirised.

What, then, I venture to assert is, that the People of Athens has no difficulty in recognising which of its citizens are of the better sort and which the opposite. And so recognising those who are serviceable and advantageous to itself, even though they be base, the People loves them; but the good folk they are disposed the rather to hate. This virtue of theirs, the People holds, is not engrained in their nature for any good to itself, but rather for its injury. In direct opposition to this, there are some persons who, being born of the People, are yet by natural instinct not commoners. For my part I pardon the People its own democracy, as, indeed, it is pardonable in any one to do good to himself. But the man who, not being himself one of the People, prefers to live in a state democratically governed rather than in an oligarchical state may be said to smooth his own path towards iniquity. He knows that a bad man has a better chance of slipping through the fingers of justice in a democratic than in an oligarchical state.

3. I repeat that my position concerning the constitution of the Athenians is this: the type of constitution is not to my taste, but given that a democratic form of government has been agreed upon, they do seem to me to go the right way to preserve the democracy by the adoption of the particular type which I have set forth.

But there are other objections brought, as I am aware, against the Athenians, by certain people, and to this effect. It not seldom happens, they tell us, that a man is unable to transact a piece of business with the senate or the People, even if he sit waiting a whole year. Now this does happen at Athens, and for no other reason save that, owing to the immense mass of affairs they are unable to work off all the business on hand and dismiss the applicants. And how in the world should they be able, considering in the first place that they, the Athenians, have more festivals to celebrate than any other state throughout the length and breadth of Hellas? . . . In the next place, only consider the number of cases they have to decide, what with private suits and public causes and scrutinies of accounts, more than the whole of the rest of mankind put together; while the senate has multifarious points to advise upon concerning peace and war, concerning ways and means, concerning the framing and passing of laws, and concerning the matters affecting the state perpetually occurring, and endless questions touching the allies; besides the receipt of the tribute, the superintendence of dockyards and temples. Can, I ask again, any one find it at all surprising that, with all these affairs on their hands, they are unequal to doing business with all the world?

But some people tell us that if the applicant will only address himself to the senate or the People with a bribe in his hand he will do a good stroke of business. And for my part I am free to confess to these gainsayers that a good many things may be done at Athens by dint of money; and I will add, that a good many more still might be done, if the money flowed still more freely and from more pockets. One thing, however, I know full well, that as to transacting with every one of these applicants all he wants, the state could not do it, not even if all the gold and silver in the world were the inducement offered.

Here are some of the cases which have to be decided on. Some one fails to fit out a ship: judgment must be given. Another puts up a building on a piece of public land: again judgment must be given. Or, to take another class of cases: adjudication has to be made between the patrons of choruses for the Dionysia, the Thargelia, the Panathenaea, the Prometheia, and the Hephaestia, year after year. Also as between the trierarchs, 400 of whom are

appointed each year, of these, too, any who choose must have
their cases adjudicated on, year after year. But that is not all.
There are various magistrates to examine and approve and decide
between; there are orphans whose status must be examined; and
guardians of prisoners to appoint. These, be it borne in mind, are
all matters of yearly occurrence; while at intervals there are
exemptions and abstentions from military service which call for
adjudication, or in connection with some other extraordinary
misdemeanour, some case of outrage and violence of an exceptional character, or some charge of impiety. A whole string of
others I simply omit; I am content to have named the most important part with the exception of the assessments of tribute
which occur, as a rule, at intervals of four years.

I put it to you, then: can any one suppose that all, or any, of
these may dispense with adjudication? If so, will any one say
which ought, and which ought not, to be adjudicated on, there
and then? If, on the other hand, we are forced to admit that
these are all fair cases for adjudication, it follows of necessity that
they should be decided during the twelve-month; since even now
the boards of judges sitting right through the year are powerless
to stay the tide of evildoing by reason of the multitude of the
people.

So far so good. "But," some one will say, "try the cases you
certainly must, but lessen the number of the judges." But if so,
it follows of necessity that unless the number of courts themselves are diminished in number there will only be a few judges
sitting in each court, with the further consequence that in dealing
with so small a body of judges it will be easier for a litigant to
present an invulnerable front to the court, and to bribe the whole
body, to the great detriment of justice.

But besides this we cannot escape the conclusion that the Athenians have their festivals to keep, during which the courts cannot
sit. As a matter of fact these festivals are twice as numerous as
those of any other people. But I will reckon them as merely equal
to those of the state which has the fewest.

This being so, I maintain that it is not possible for business
affairs at Athens to stand on any very different footing from the
present, except to some slight extent, by adding here and deduct-
ing there. Any large modification is out of the question, short

of damaging the democracy itself. No doubt many expedients might be discovered for improving the constitution, but if the problem be to discover some adequate means of improving the constitution, while at the same time the democracy is to remain intact, I say it is not easy to do this, except, as I have just stated, to the extent of some trifling addition here or deduction there.

There is another point in which it is sometimes felt that the Athenians are ill advised, in their adoption, namely, of the less respectable party, in a state divided by faction. But if so, they do it advisedly. If they chose the more respectable, they would be adopting those whose views and interests differ from their own, for there is no state in which the best element is friendly to the people. It is the worst element which in every state favours the democracy—on the principle that like favours like. It is simple enough then. The Athenians choose what is most akin to themselves. Also on every occasion on which they have attempted to side with the better classes, it has not fared well with them, but within a short interval the democratic party has been enslaved, as for instance in Boeotia; or, as when they chose the aristocrats of the Milesians, and within a short time these revolted and cut the people to pieces; or, as when they chose the Lacedaemonians as against the Messenians, and within a short time the Lacedaemonians subjugated the Messenians and went to war against Athens.

I seem to overhear a retort, "No one, of course, is deprived of his civil rights at Athens unjustly." My answer is, that there are some who are unjustly deprived of their civil rights, though the cases are certainly rare. But it will take more than a few to attack the democracy at Athens, since you may take it as an established fact, it is not the man who has lost his civil rights justly that takes the matter to heart, but the victims, if any, of injustice. But how in the world can any one imagine that many are in a state of civil disability at Athens, where the People and the holders of office are one and the same? It is from iniquitous exercise of office, from iniquity exhibited either in speech or action, and the like circumstances, that citizens are punished with deprivation of civil rights in Athens. Due reflection on these matters will serve to dispel the notion that there is any danger at Athens from persons visited with disfranchisement.

PLATO: SELECTIONS

3 Epistles

It is impossible to compress Plato's views of democracy into one selection; therefore, a few comments on the development of his thought are necessary. Born in the fourth year of the Peloponnesian War, Plato reached manhood in an Athens wrenched by the abnormal pressures and internal dissension created by that conflict. Granted that a democracy at war does not always present its best face, even so Plato's natural temperament, his idealism, his ferocious intelligence, and—it should be admitted—his aristocratic family background, led him to see the defects of popular sovereignty all the more keenly. His views on the Athenian democracy shortly after its restoration in the first years of the fourth century can be seen nowhere so clearly as in his own words:

The more I reflected upon what was happening, upon what kind of men were active in politics, and upon the state of our laws and customs, and the older I grew, the more I realized how difficult it is to manage a city's affairs rightly. For I saw it was impossible to do anything without friends and loyal followers; and to find such men ready to hand would be a piece of sheer good luck, since our city was no longer guided by the customs and practices of our fathers, while to train up new ones was

SOURCE. From Plato, *Epistles*, Glenn R. Morrow, tr., Indianapolis: The Bobbs-Merrill Company, Inc., Publishers, 1962, from Epistle vii. Copyright 1962 by The Bobbs-Merrill Company, Inc. Reprinted by permission of the publishers.

anything but easy. And the corruption of our written laws and our customs was proceeding at such amazing speed that whereas at first I had been full of zeal for public life, when I noted these changes and saw how unstable everything was, I became in the end quite dizzy; and though I did not cease to reflect how an improvement could be brought about in our laws and in the whole constitution, yet I refrained from action, waiting for the proper time. At last I came to the conclusion that all existing states are badly governed and the condition of their laws practically incurable, without some miraculous remedy and the assistance of fortune; and I was forced to say, in praise of true philosophy, that from her height alone was it possible to discern what the nature of justice is, either in the state or in the individual, and that the ills of the human race would never end until either those who are sincerely and truly lovers of wisdom come into political power, or the rulers of our cities, by the grace of God, learn true philosophy.

4 Gorgias

In a later work, the Gorgias *(often thought to be Plato's rationale for not having entered public life), Plato clarifies his concept of the state. The true goal of any government is not to cater to the material prosperity of its citizens (as a chef caters to the physical desires), but to improve their wisdom and virtue (as a physician caters to physical needs).*

In the Gorgias, *when a comparison is being made between contemporary and former Athenian statesmen, Plato has Socrates criticize the previous generation as follows:*

SOURCE. From Plato, *Gorgias*, W. C. Helmbold, tr., Indianapolis: The Liberal Arts Press, 1952, 517b–519a. Copyright 1952 by The Liberal Arts Press, Inc. Reprinted by permission of the Liberal Arts Press Division of The Bobbs-Merrill Company, Inc.

They seem to me, in fact, to have been more serviceable than the present generation, and more capable of giving the state what it wanted. But as for transforming its desires instead of toadying to them, as for persuading and coercing fellow citizens to the point of self-improvement, there is not, in a word, a whit of difference between generations. Yet this and this alone is the task of a truly good citizen. I freely acknowledge that the former age was cleverer at providing ships and walls and docks and the rest of it than are our contemporaries. . . .

You came along with the opinion that there have been good and honest citizens in the state. When I ventured to ask you who they may be—look at the politicians you brought up![1] Do you know what seems to me to have the closest resemblance to them? It's just as though I should question you about physical culture and asked what men have been, or are, good trainers of the body and you were to answer in all seriousness, "Thearion the baker, and Mithaecus who wrote the treatise on Sicilian cookery, and Sarambus the shopkeeper: these have been wonderful physical trainers, since the first makes marvelous bread, the second cooks well, and the third provides excellent wine." And perhaps you would be offended if I were to say to you, "Man alive, you have no comprehension of true physical culture! You're merely listing servile fellows who cater to the appetites and have no understanding of the fine points." . . . And what you are now doing, Callicles, is something extremely similar: you praise men who wined and dined our fellow citizens and crammed them full of what they desired. Men say that they made our city great, not perceiving that it is swollen and ulcerous because of its ancient counselors. With no regard for self-control or justice they stuffed our state with harbors and docks and walls and tribute money and all such nonsense; so when . . . illness finally comes, they will blame the advisers who happen to be around at the time, while praising to the skies Themistocles and Cimon and Pericles, though they were the true authors of the trouble.

---

[1] Socrates' opponent, Callicles, had mentioned the names of four of Athens' greatest statesmen and benefactors: Miltiades, Themistocles, Cimon, and Pericles. *Ed.*

5 *The Republic*

Implied in this argument is the inherent failure of democracy, as Plato saw it. If the goal of the statesman is to improve the citizens, then any government based on popular sovereignty must inevitably fail. For the common man is not prepared by education and temperament to perceive virtue; therefore, he will give his loyalty to statesmen who cater to his baser appetites and pamper him with materialistic rewards to improve his physical lot, and flattering oratory to improve his self-esteem.

In the dialogue Statesman, *Plato further defines the three types of government. There are three ideal forms: monarchy, aristocracy, and constitutional democracy (in which the temper of the popular assembly is moderated by inviolable laws). These ideal forms have their corrupt counterparts: tyranny, oligarchy, and the sort of lawless democracy in which the popular assembly is sovereign and free from constitutional restraint. True statesmanship is a seventh form, distinct from these six, and is said to stand in the same relationship to these governments as God does to man. Plato does admit that while constitutional democracy may be the worst of all three ideal forms, lawless democracy is also the least offensive of the three corrupt forms. In fact, it should be remembered that Plato reserved his most savage criticism for the despot, or the tyranny of an oligarchy; his contempt for democracy can at least be tinged with good humor, as we see in this passage of the* Republic:

"Then democracy originates when the poor win, kill or exile their opponents, and give the rest equal rights and opportunities of office, appointment to office being as a rule by lot."

"Yes," he agreed, "that is how a democracy is established,

SOURCE. Plato, *The Republic* (VIII, 557a–558c), H. D. P. Lee, ed. and tr., Middlesex, England: Penguin Books, Ltd., 1955. Copyright 1955. Reprinted by permission of Penguin Books, Ltd.

whether it's done by force of arms or by frightening its opponents into retreat."

"What sort of a society will it be?" I asked, "and how will it be run? The answer, obviously, will show us the character of the democratic man."

"Obviously."

"Would you agree, first, that people will be free? There is liberty and freedom of speech in plenty, and every individual is free to do as he likes."

"That's what they say."

"That being so, won't everyone arrange his life as pleases him best?"

"Obviously."

"And so there will be the greatest variety of individual character?"

"There's bound to be."

"I dare say that a democracy is the most attractive of all societies," I said. "The diversity of its characters, like the different colours in a patterned dress, make it look very attractive. Indeed," I added, "perhaps most people would, for this reason, judge it to be the best form of society, like women and children who judge by appearances."

"Very likely."

"And, you know, it's just the place to go constitution-hunting. It contains every possible type, because of the wide freedom it allows, and anyone engaged in founding a state, as we are doing, should perhaps be made to pay a visit to a democracy and make his choice from the variety of models it displays, before he proceeds to make his own foundation."

"It's a shop in which he'd find plenty of models on show."

"Then in democracy," I went on, "there's no compulsion either to exercise authority if you are capable of it, or to submit to authority if you don't want to; you needn't fight if there's a war, or you can wage a private war in peacetime if you don't like peace; and if there's any law that debars you from political or judicial office, you will none the less take either if they come your way. It's a wonderfully pleasant way of carrying on in the short run, isn't it?"

"In the short run perhaps."

"And isn't there something rather charming about the good-temper of those who've been sentenced in court? You must have noticed that in a democracy men sentenced to death or exile continue, none the less, to go about among their fellows, who take no more notice of them than if they were invisible spirits."

"I've often seen that."

"Then they're very considerate in applying the high principles we laid down when founding our state; so far from interpreting them strictly, they really look down on them. We said that no one who had not exceptional gifts could grow into a good man unless he were brought up from childhood in a good environment and given a good training; democracy with a grandiose gesture sweeps all this away and doesn't mind what the habits and background of its politicians are, provided they profess themselves the people's friends."

"All very splendid."

"These, then, and similar characteristics are those of democracy. It's an agreeable, anarchic form of society, with plenty of variety, which treats all men as equal, whether they are equal or not."

"The picture is easy to recognize."

ARISTOTLE: SELECTIONS

The greatest intellect of antiquity was born in one of the back-waters of Greek civilization, the little town of Stageira in Macedon, but it was his achievements as a scholar and teacher in Athens that brought him fame during his lifetime and insured his immortality. As a student in Plato's Academy (367–347), he mastered the principles of dialectic and the insistence of the Academy upon definition. After Plato's death he founded his own school, the Lyceum, and took upon himself no lesser task than the organization of the entire corpus of human wisdom into separate disciplines. It is obvious to the most casual reader that Aristotle is more of this world than is Plato; he is empirical rather than idealistic, and as far as scholarly method is concerned, he tended, in every field of knowledge, to observe, to collect masses of data, and only then to formulate first principles, while Plato too often regarded first principles as self-evident. This is a common generalization made about the thought of Plato and Aristotle and it must be confessed that it is a dangerous oversimplification. For not even Aristotle could escape the temptation to create abstract principles from insufficient data. His method, in more scientific fields, is difficult to fault even today, but when he attempts to reduce such an amorphous subject as the entire human political experience to orderly exposition, his fatal fondness for symmetry and organization becomes immediately apparent.

Aristotle accepted the Academy's terminology as the basis for all political analysis: all states are either monarchies, aristocracies, democracies, or corruptions of these forms. Therefore, when he collected the histories of 158 constitutions of various states, in preparation for the composition of The Politics, *he tended to see these states as collections of predictable institutions rather than groups of unpredictable human beings. Nowhere is this clearer than in his treatment of Athens. For while his* Constitution of Athens *was evidently com-*

piled before The Politics *was written, and was intended to be only part of the evidence used in reaching the conclusions of* The Politics, *it is obvious that the history of Athenian government contained in the previous work was interpreted according to preconceived notions of how governments work: facts are made to fit theories throughout; the "better classes" are distinguished from the masses; a century of Athenian political development is forced into a spectrum of forms in which institutions change from "aristocratic" to "democratic" with little concern for the vast sociological and psychological changes taking place within Athenian society during this era.*

Many of Aristotle's theories about democracy are revealed in the following selections from The Politics. *He believed that the masses were capable of a sort of corporate wisdom, but their decision-making should be limited to situations not already covered by wise and immutable laws. This is the best kind of democracy, and within its framework all classes will have equal influence without regard to their actual numbers. In other words, the number of rich men will be much smaller than the number of poor men, but rich and poor will have equal influence (note that Aristotle seems to believe that men's interests will be determined by their incomes). In the worst type of democracy, constitutional law is disregarded and the popular assembly rules from day to day by decree.*

Democracies will also vary according to the types of population. Small farmers are best, for they own property and do not have the leisure to come into town and attend the assemblies. A large urban population is worst because the poor will soon gain the upper hand and begin to redistribute the wealth.

6   *The Politics*

§ 1. The other alternatives may be reserved for a later inquiry; but the first of the alternatives suggested—that the people at large

SOURCE. From *The Politics of Aristotle*, Ernest Barker, ed. and tr., New York: Oxford University Press, 1962, pp. 123–127; 167–169; 258–269. Reprinted by permission of Oxford University Press.

should be sovereign rather than the few best—would appear to be
defensible, and while it presents some difficulty it perhaps also
contains some truth.   § 2. There is this to be said for the Many.
Each of them by himself may not be of a good quality; but when
they all come together it is possible that they may surpass—
collectively and as a body, although not individually—the quality
of the few best. Feasts to which many contribute may excel those
provided at one man's expense. In the same way, when there are
many [who contribute to the process of deliberation], each can
bring his share of goodness and moral prudence; and when all
meet together the people may thus become something in the nature
of a single person, who—as he has many feet, many hands, and
many senses—may also have many qualities of character and intelligence.   § 3. This is the reason why the Many are also better
judges [than the few] of music and the writings of poets: some
appreciate one part, some another, and all together appreciate all.
§ 4. [We may note that this combination of qualities, which gives
the Many their merit, can also be traced in cases of *individual*
merit.] The thing which makes a good man differ from a unit
in the crowd—as it is also the thing which is generally said to
make a beautiful person differ from one who is not beautiful, or
an artistic representation differ from ordinary reality—is that elements which are elsewhere scattered and separate are here combined in a unity. [It is this unity which counts]; for if you take
the elements separately, you may say of an artistic representation
that it is surpassed by the eye of this person or by some other
feature of that.

§ 5.   It is not clear, however, that this combination of qualities,
which we have made the ground of distinction between the many
and the few best, is true of all popular bodies and all large masses
of men. Perhaps it may be said, "By heaven, it is clear that there
are some bodies of which it cannot possibly be true; for if you
included them, you would, by the same token, be bound to include
a herd of beasts. That would be absurd; and yet what difference
is there between these bodies and a herd of beasts?" All the same,
and in spite of this objection, there is nothing to prevent the view
we have stated from being true of *some* popular bodies.

§ 6. It would thus seem possible to solve, by the considerations we have advanced, both the problem raised in the previous chapter "What body of *persons* should be sovereign?" and the further problem which follows upon it, "What are the *matters* over which freemen, or the general body of citizens—men of the sort who neither have wealth nor can make any claim on the ground of goodness—should properly exercise sovereignty?" § 7. It may be argued, from one point of view, that it is dangerous for men of this sort to share in the highest offices, as injustice may lead them into wrongdoing, and thoughtlessness into error. But it may also be argued, from another point of view, that there is serious risk in not letting them have *some* share in the enjoyment of power; for a state with a body of disfranchised citizens who are numerous and poor must necessarily be a state which is full of enemies. § 8. The alternative left is to let them share in the deliberative and judicial functions; and we thus find Solon, and some of the other legislators, giving the people the two general functions of electing the magistrates to office and of calling them to account at the end of their tenure of office, but *not* the right of holding office themselves in their individual capacity. § 9. [There is wisdom in such a policy.] When they all meet together, the people display a good enough gift of perception, and combined with the better class they are of service to the state (just as impure food, when it is mixed with pure, makes the whole concoction more nutritious than a small amount of the pure would be); but each of them is imperfect in the judgements he forms by himself.

§ 10. But this arrangement of the constitution [which gives the people deliberative and judicial functions] presents some difficulties. The first difficulty is that it may well be held that the function of judging when medical attendance has been properly given [a function analogous to that of the people in judging the conduct of magistrates] should belong to those whose profession it is to attend patients and cure the complaints from which they suffer—in a word, to members of the medical profession. The same may be held to be true of all other professions and arts; and just as doctors should have their conduct examined before a body of doctors, so, too, should those who follow other professions have theirs examined before a body of members of their own profession. § 11. [We may note, however, that] the term "doctor" is used in three different senses. It is applied to the ordinary practitioner: it is applied to the specialist who directs the course of treatment; and it is also applied to the man who has some general knowledge of the art of medicine. (There are men of this last type to be found in connexion with nearly all the arts; and we credit them with the power of judging as much as we do the experts—i.e. the practitioners and specialists.) § 12. When we turn to consider the matter of election [as distinct from examination], the same principles would appear to apply. To make a proper election, it may be argued, is equally the work of experts. It is the work of those who are versed in geometry to choose a geometrician, or, again, of those who are acquainted with steering to choose a steersman; and even if, in some occupations and arts, there are some nonexperts who also share in the ability to choose, they do not share in a higher degree than the experts. § 13. It would thus appear, on this line of argument, that the people should not be made sovereign, either in the matter of the election of magistrates or in that of their examination. § 14. It may be, however, that these arguments are not altogether well founded. In the first place we have to remember our own previous argument of the combination of qualities which is to be found in the people—provided, that is to say, that they are not debased in character. Each individual may indeed, be a worse judge than the experts; but all, when they meet together, are either better than experts or at any rate no worse. In the second place, there are a number of arts in which the creative artist is not the only, or even the best, judge. These are the arts whose products can be understood and judged even by those who do not possess any skill in the art. A house, for instance, is something which can be understood by others besides the builder: indeed the user of a house—or in other words the householder—will judge it even better than he does. In the same way a pilot will judge a rudder better than a shipwright does; and the diner—not the cook—will be the best judge of a feast.

§ 15. The first difficulty which confronts our argument about the rights of the people would appear to be answered sufficiently by these considerations. But there is a second difficulty still to be faced, which is connected with the first. It would seem to be

absurd that persons of a poor quality should be sovereign on
issues which are more important than those assigned to the better
sort of citizens. The election of magistrates, and their examination
at the end of their tenure, are the most important of issues; and
yet there are constitutions, as we have seen, under which these
issues are assigned to popular bodies, and where a popular body
is sovereign in all such matters. § 16. To add to the difficulty,
membership of the assembly, which carries deliberative and
judicial functions, is vested in persons of little property and of
any age; but a high property qualification is demanded from those
who serve as treasurers or generals, or hold any of the highest
offices. This difficulty too may, however, be met in the same way
as the first; and the practice followed in these constitutions is
perhaps, after all, correct. § 17. It is not the individual member
of the judicial court, or the council, or the assembly, who is vested
with office: it is the court as a whole, the council as a whole, the
popular assembly as a whole, which is vested; and each individual
member—whether of the council, the assembly, or the court—is
simply a part of the whole. § 18. It is therefore just and proper
that the people, from which the assembly, the council, and the
court are constituted, should be sovereign on issues more important
than those assigned to the better sort of citizens. It may be added
that the collective property of the members of all these bodies is
greater than that of the persons who either as individuals or as
members of small bodies hold the highest [executive] offices.

§ 19. This may serve as a settlement of the difficulties which
have been discussed. But the discussion of the first of these difficulties [whether expert skill or general knowledge should be
the sovereign authority] leads to one conclusion above all others.
Rightly constituted laws should be the final sovereign; and personal rule, whether it be exercised by a single person or a body
of persons, should be sovereign only in those matters on which
law is unable, owing to the difficulty of framing general rules
for all contingencies, to make an exact pronouncement. § 20. But
what rightly constituted laws ought to be is a matter that is not
yet clear; and here we are still confronted by the difficulty stated
at the end of the previous chapter—that law itself may have a
bias in favour of one class or another. Equally with the constitu-

tions to which they belong [and *according to* the constitutions to which they belong] laws must be good or bad, just or unjust. § 21. The one clear fact is that laws must be constituted in accordance with constitutions; and if this is the case, it follows that laws which are in accordance with right constitutions must necessarily be just, and laws which are in accordance with wrong or perverted constitutions must be unjust. [from bk. III. 1281–82]

§ 20. The fact that there are a number of constitutions, and the causes of that fact, have already been established. We may now go on to say that there are also a number of varieties of two of these constitutions—democracy and oligarchy. This is already clear from what has been previously said. . . . § 21. These constitutions vary because the people (*dēmos*) and the class called the notables vary. So far as the people are concerned, one sort is engaged in farming; a second is engaged in the arts and crafts; a third is the marketing sort, which is engaged in buying and selling; a fourth is the maritime sort, which in turn is partly naval, partly mercantile, partly employed on ferries, and partly engaged in fisheries. . . . A fifth sort is composed of unskilled labourers and persons whose means are too small to enable them to enjoy any leisure; a sixth consists of those who are not of free birth by two citizen parents; and there may also be other sorts of a similar character. § 22. The notables fall into different sorts according to wealth, birth, merit, culture, and other qualities of the same order.

The first variety of democracy is the variety which is said to follow the principle of equality closest. In this variety the law declares equality to mean that the poor are to count no more than the rich: neither is to be sovereign, and both are to be on a level. § 23. [We may approve this law]; for if we hold, as some thinkers do, that liberty and equality are chiefly to be found in democracy, it will be along these lines—with all sharing alike, as far as possible, in constitutional rights—that they will most likely be found. A constitution of this order is bound to be a democracy; for [while all share alike] the people are the majority, and the will of the majority is sovereign. § 24. A second variety of democracy is that in which offices are assigned on the basis of a property qualification, but the qualification is low: those who attain it have to be admitted to a share in office, and those who lose it are excluded. A third variety is one in which every citizen of unimpeachable descent can share in office, but the law is the final sovereign. § 25. A fourth variety is one in which every person [irrespective of descent, and] provided only that he is a citizen, can share in office, but the law is still the final sovereign. A fifth variety of democracy is like the fourth in admitting to office every person who has the status of citizen; but here the people, and not the law, is the final sovereign. This is what happens when popular decrees are sovereign instead of the law; and that is a result which is brought about by leaders of the demagogue type. § 26. In democracies which obey the law there are no demagogues; it is the better class of citizens who preside over affairs. Demagogues arise in states where the laws are not sovereign. The people then becomes an autocrat—a single composite autocrat made up of many members, with the many playing the sovereign, not as individuals, but collectively. § 27. It is not clear what Homer means when he says that "it is not good to have the rule of many masters": whether he has in mind the collective rule of the many, or the rule of a number of magistrates acting as individuals. However that may be, a democracy of this order, being in the nature of an autocrat and not being governed by law, begins to attempt an autocracy. It grows despotic; flatterers come to be held in honour; it becomes analogous to the tyrannical form of single-person government. § 28. Both show a similar temper; both behave like despots to the better class of citizens; the decrees of the one are like the edicts of the other; the popular leader in the one is the same as, or at any rate like, the flatterer in the other; and in either case the influence of favourites predominates—that of the flatterer in tyrannies, and that of the popular leader in democracies of this variety. § 29. It is popular leaders who, by referring all issues to the decision of the people, are responsible for substituting the sovereignty of decrees for that of the laws. Once the people are sovereign in all matters, *they* are sovereign themselves over its decisions; the multitude follows their guidance; and this is the source of their great position. § 30. But the critics of the magistrates are also responsible. Their argument is, "The *people* ought to decide": the people accept that invitation readily; and thus the authority of all the magistrates is undermined. There would appear to be solid substance in the view that a democracy of this type is not a true constitution. Where the laws are not sovereign, there is no constitution. § 31. Law should be sovereign on every issue, and the magistrates and the citizen body should only decide about details. The conclusion which emerges is clear. Democracy may be a form of constitution; but this particular system, under which everything is managed merely by decrees, is not even a democracy, in any real sense of the word. Decrees can never be general rules [and any real constitution must be based on general rules]. . . . So far, then, as concerns the different forms of democracy, and the definition of those forms. . . . [from bk. IV, 1291–92]

§ 1. The underlying idea of the democratic type of constitution is liberty. (This, it is commonly said, can only be enjoyed in democracy; and this, it is also said, is the aim of every democracy.) Liberty has more than one form. One of its forms [is the political, which] consists in the interchange of ruling and being ruled. § 2. The democratic conception of justice is the enjoyment of arithmetical equality, and not the enjoyment of proportionate equality on the basis of desert. On this arithmetical conception of justice the masses must necessarily be sovereign; the will of the majority must be ultimate and must be the expression of justice. The argument is that each citizen should be on an equality with the rest; and the result which follows in democracies is that the poor—they being in a majority, and the will of the majority being sovereign—are more sovereign than the rich. § 3. Such is the first form of liberty, which all democrats agree in making the aim of their sort of constitution. The other form [is the civil, which] consists in "living as you like." Such a life, the democrats argue, is the function of the free man, just as the function of slaves is *not* to live as they like. § 4. This is the second aim of democracy. Its issue is, ideally, freedom from any interference of government, and, failing that, such freedom as comes from the interchange of ruling and being ruled. It contributes, in this way, to a general system of liberty based on equality.

§ 5. Such being the idea of democracy, and the root from which it develops, we can now proceed to study its attributes or institutions. [Under the head of the executive], there is the election of officers *by* all, and *from* all; there is the system of all ruling over each, and each, in his turn, over all; there is the method of appointing by lot to all offices—or, at any rate, to all which do not require some practical experience and professional skill; there is the rule that there should be no property-qualification for office—or, at any rate, the lowest possible; there is the rule that, apart from the military offices, no office should ever be held twice by the same person—or, at any rate, only on few occasions, and those relating only to a few offices; there is, finally, the rule that the tenure of every office—or, at any rate, of as many as possible—should be brief. [Under the head of the judicature], there is the system of popular courts, composed of all the citizens or of persons selected from all, and competent to decide all cases—or, at any rate, most of them, and those the greatest and most important, such as the audit of official accounts, constitutional issues, and matters of contract. [Under the head of the deliberative] there is the rule that the popular assembly should be sovereign in all matters—or, at any rate, in the most important; and conversely that the executive magistracies should be sovereign in none—or, at any rate, in as few as possible.

§ 6. Among the executive magistracies the one most popular in democracies is the Council, wherever there are not adequate means for paying all the citizens to attend the popular assembly. If there *are* adequate means, the Council itself is deprived of its power; and the people, once it is furnished with pay, begins to take everything into its hands. . . . § 7. This system of payment is a further attribute of democracy. The ideal is payment in every sphere—popular assembly, courts, and executive magistracies; but if that cannot be had, there will at any rate be payment for attending the courts, the council, and the stated meetings of the popular assembly, and also for serving on any board of magistrates—or, at the least, any board whose members are required to have a common table. (It may be remarked that while oligarchy is characterized by good birth, wealth, and culture, the attributes of democracy would appear to be the very opposite—low birth,

poverty, and vulgarity.)   § 8. Another attribute of democracy
is to dispense with all life offices—or at least to curtail the powers
of any such offices, if they have been left surviving from some
earlier epoch of change, and to make. appointments to any life-
office depend on the use of the lot and not on election.

§ 9. These are the attributes common to democracies generally.
But if we look at the form of democracy and the sort of populace
which is generally held to be specially typical, we have to connect
it [not so much with these attributes, as] with the conception of
justice which is the recognized democratic conception—that of
equality of rights for all on an arithmetical basis. Equality here
might be taken to mean that the poorer class should exercise no
greater authority than the rich, or, in other words, that sovereignty should not be exercised only by it, but equally vested in all
the citizens on a numerical basis. If that were the interpretation
followed, the upholders of democracy could afford to believe that
equality—and liberty—was really achieved by their constitution. . . .

To find theoretically where truth resides, in these matters of
equality and justice, is a very difficult task. Difficult as it may
be, it is an easier task than that of persuading men to act justly,
if they have power enough to secure their own selfish interests.
The weaker are always anxious for equality and justice. The
strong pay no heed to either.

§ 1. Of the four varieties of democracy the best, as has already
been noted in the previous section of our inquiry, is the one that
comes first in the order of classification. It is also the oldest of all
the varieties. But the reason why it comes first is not that: it is a
reason connected with the grading of the different kinds of populace. The first and best kind of populace is one of farmers; and
there is thus no difficulty in constructing a democracy where the
bulk of the people live by arable or pastoral farming.   § 2. Such
people, not having any great amount of property, are busily occupied; and they have thus no time for attending the assembly. Not
possessing the necessities of life, they stick to their work, and do
not covet what does not belong to them; indeed they find more
pleasure in work than they do in politics and government—unless
there are large pickings to be got from having a finger in govern-

ment. § 3. The masses covet profits more than they covet honours; witness the patience with which they bore the old-time tyrannies, and still continue to tolerate oligarchies if only they are allowed to get on with their work and are not robbed of their earnings. Give them the chance and they soon make their way—either up into riches, or, at any rate, out of poverty. § 4. Any craving which the masses may feel for position and power will be satisfied if they are given the right of electing magistrates and calling them to account. Indeed there are instances which show that the masses will be contented with a still smaller measure of power. We may cite the example of Mantinea, where the people did not enjoy the right of electing the magistrates (it was vested instead in persons selected from the body of the people on a system of rotation), but exercised, at any rate, the power of deliberation. § 5. Such a system [even if it gives only limited power to the people] must still be considered as a system of democracy, and it was such at Mantinea.

On these general grounds we may argue that policy, as well as general practice, suggests a system of balance in the first [i.e. the agricultural] variety of democracy. On the one hand all the citizens will enjoy the three rights of electing the magistrates, calling them to account, and sitting in the law courts; on the other hand the most important offices will be filled by election, and confined to those who can satisfy a property qualification. The greater the importance of an office, the greater might be the property qualification required. Alternatively, no property qualification might be required for any office, but only men of capacity would actually be appointed. § 6. A state which is governed in this way will be sure to be well governed (its offices will always be in the hands of the best of its members, with the people giving its consent and bearing no grudge against persons of quality); and the men of quality and the notables will be sure to be satisfied, under a system which at once preserves them from being governed by other and inferior persons and ensures (by giving others the right to call them to account) that they will themselves govern justly. § 7. To be kept in such dependence, and to be denied the power of doing just as he pleases, is an advantage to any man. The power of acting at will leaves men with no defence against the evil impulses present in all of us. Where there is responsibility, the result must always be an advantage of the first order in any constitution: government will be conducted by men of quality, and they will be saved from misconduct, while the masses will have their just rights. . . .

§ 11. Next to a populace of farmers, the best sort [as a basis for democracy] is a pastoral populace living by its herds and flocks. Many of their characteristics are similar to those of farmers; but with their robust physique, and their capacity for camping out in the open, they are specially trained and hardened into a good condition for war. § 12. The other kinds of populace, which form the basis of the other varieties of democracy, are almost without exception of a much poorer stamp. They lead a poor sort of life: and none of the occupations followed by a populace which consists of mechanics, shop-keepers, and day labourers, leaves any room for excellence. § 13. Revolving round the market-place and the city centre, people of this class generally find it easy to attend the sessions of the popular assembly—unlike the farmers who, scattered through the country-side, neither meet so often nor feel so much the need for society of this sort. § 14. When [in addition to a populace of farmers or pastoralists] there is also the further advantage of a country-side which lies at a considerable distance from the city, it is easy to construct a good democracy or a good "polity." The mass of the people are then compelled to fix their abode outside the city, on their lands; and even if there is still a mob left which lives round the market-place, a rule will have to be made, where the constitution is democratic, that there shall be no meetings of the populace assembly which cannot be attended by all the inhabitants of the country-side. . . .

The last variety, which includes all classes alike, is one that cannot be borne by all states, and can hardly itself endure, unless it is properly constituted in point of laws and customs. The causes which lead to the destruction of this as of other forms of government have already been, in the main, described [in the previous book]. § 16. In attempting its construction the leaders of popular parties usually follow the policy of seeking to strengthen the populace by simply increasing its numbers to the utmost possible extent. Citizenship is given not only to the law-fully born, but also to the illegitimate; it is given to those who have only one citizen parent, whether that parent be father or mother: in fact there is nothing of this order but will serve, in such a state, as so much grist for "the people." § 17. But if this is the policy of construction usually followed by demagogues, the policy which ought to be followed is different. Increase of numbers should stop at the point at which the masses just exceed the combined strength of the notables and the middle class. It should never go beyond this point. Any greater proportion will at once disturb the balance of the constitution; and it will also incite the notables to chafe still more against democracy—a state of feeling which led to the revolution in Cyrene. A small evil may be overlooked; but an evil which grows to large dimensions is always before men's eyes. § 18. Other measures which are also useful in constructing this last and most extreme type of democracy are measures like those introduced by Cleisthenes at Athens, when he sought to advance the cause of democracy, or those which were taken by the founders of popular government at Cyrene. § 19. This means that a number of new tribes and clans should be instituted by the side of the old; that private cults should be reduced in number and conducted at common centres; and that every contrivance should be employed to make all the citizens mix, as much as they possibly can, and to break down their old loyalties. § 20. The measures adopted by tyrants may equally be regarded as all congenial to democracy [in its extreme form]. We may cite as an instance the license allowed to slaves (which, up to a point, may be advantageous as well as congenial), and the license permitted to women and children. We may also cite the policy of connivance at the practice of "living as you like." Such a policy ensures a large body of support for the constitution in which it is followed. Most men find more pleasure in living without any discipline than they find in a life of temperance.

§ 1. Legislators and would-be founders of any constitution of this type [i.e. the type of extreme democracy] will find that the work of construction is not their only or principal business. The maintenance of a constitution is the thing which really matters. A state may last for two or three days under any kind of constitution; [the real test is the test of survival]. § 2. Legislators should therefore direct their attention to the causes which lead to the preservation and the destruction of constitutions—a theme which has already been treated—and on that basis they should devote their effort to the construction of stability. They must be on their guard against all the elements of destruction; they must leave their state with a body of laws, customary as well as enacted, which will include, above everything else, all the elements of preservation; they must believe that the true policy, for democracy and oligarchy alike, is not one which ensures the greatest possible amount of either, but one which will ensure the longest possible life for both. § 3. The demagogues of our own day, zealous to please the peoples of their states, cause a large amount of property to be confiscated to public use by means of the law courts. Those who care for the well-being of their constitution should labour to correct such practices. They should have a law passed which prevents the fines imposed in law courts from becoming public property or being paid into the treasury, and makes them, instead of that, temple-property. Wrong-doers would not, in that case, be any more heedless than they are now (they would still have to pay the same fine), and the people, having nothing to gain, would be less inclined to condemn all defendants. § 4. Public prosecutions should also be made as few as possible; and heavy fines should be used to deter prosecutors from bringing them at random. Such prosecutions are usually brought against notables only, and not against those who belong to the popular party; but the proper policy, wherever it can be pursued, is to keep all citizens alike attached to the constitution and the government under it, or at any rate, failing that, to prevent any citizen from regarding the government as his enemy.

§ 5. Extreme democracies are generally to be found in populous states, where it is difficult to get the citizens to attend the popular assembly without a system of payment. Such a system bears hardly on the notables—unless a state has already in hand sufficient revenues to pay its cost. The necessary funds have to be procured by a tax on property, by confiscation, and through the agency of bad law courts; and these are all methods which have led in the past to the overthrow of many democracies. This suggests that, unless there are sufficient revenues already in hand, the meetings of the popular assembly should be infrequent, and the number of sittings of the popular law courts should be as small as their membership is large. § 6. If the sittings of the courts are thus restricted, two advantages will ensue. In the first place, the wealthier classes will cease to fear the expenditure involved—the more if it is only the poor, and not also the well-to-do, who are allowed to receive any pay; and secondly, the cases before the courts will be much better decided, as the rich (who do not care to be absent from their business for days together, but do not mind a short absence) will now be willing to attend. § 7. When, on the other hand, a state has sufficient revenues to defray the cost of a system of payment, [they should be husbanded for that purpose, and] the policy nowadays followed by demagogues should be avoided. It is their habit to distribute any surplus among the people; and the people, in the act of taking, ask for the same again. To help the poor in this way is to fill a leaky jar. . . . Yet it is the duty of a genuine democrat to see to it that the masses are not excessively poor. § 8. Poverty is the cause of the defects of democracy. That is the reason why measures should be taken to ensure a permanent level of prosperity. This is in the interest of all classes, including the prosperous themselves; and therefore the proper policy is to accumulate any surplus revenue in a fund, and then to distribute this fund in block grants to the poor. The ideal method of distribution, if a sufficient fund can be accumulated, is to make such grants sufficient for the purchase of a plot of land: failing that, they should be large enough to start men in commerce or agriculture. § 9. If such grants cannot be made to all the poor simultaneously, they should be distributed successively, by tribes or other divisions: and meanwhile the rich should contribute a sum sufficient to provide the poor with payment for their attendance at the obligatory meetings of the assembly, and should be excused, in return, from the rendering of useless public services [such as the equipping of choruses at dramatic festivals]. [from bk. VI, 1317–20]

7   Constitution of Athens

In this selection from the Constitution of Athens *Aristotle shows
how a "good" democracy developed into a "bad" one. It is interesting
to note that the steps followed are exactly those outlined in* The
Politics. *First, the urban population grows proportionally larger. Then
the body responsible for enforcing the constitutional laws (represented here by the Council of the Areopagus) is weakened and its
powers are distributed to the people's assemblies and courts. With
this safeguard removed, the people no longer listen to the better
class of leader but begin to choose demagogues who corrupt orderly
government.*

(c. 594) Solon also established a Council of Four Hundred,
one hundred from each tribe. Yet he still made it the task of the
Areopagus to watch over the laws, just as in the preceding period
it had been the guardian of the political order; and this Council
[that is, the Areopagus] still supervised the greater and more
important part of public life and, in particular, chastised offenders,
with full power to impose punishment and fines. . . . It also tried
those who had conspired to deprive the people of their political
rights, Solon having enacted a law of impeachment for such cases.

(511–508) After the overthrow of the tyranny, Isagoras, the
son of Tisander, a former supporter of the tyrants, and Cleisthenes from the family of the Alcmeonidae pitted their respective
political strengths and influences against each other. When Cleisthenes was defeated in the political clubs, he won the support of
the common people by promising to give the state into their
hands. . . . After the political power had come into the hands of

SOURCE. From Aristotle's *Constitution of Athens*, Kurt von Fritz and
Ernst Kapp, ed. and tr., New York: Hafner Publishing Co., Inc., 1950,
pp. 76, 89–91, 93–99, and 113–114. Reprinted by permission of Hafner Publishing Co., Inc.

the people in this way, Cleisthenes became their chief and "the leader of the people."[1]

. . . So then, being the leader of the people, in the fourth year after the overthrow of the tyranny, . . . he distributed the whole population into ten tribes instead of the previous four, with the aim of mixing up the population so that a greater number would share in the administration of the state . . .[2] Then he established a Council of Five Hundred instead of the existing one of Four Hundred, taking fifty from each tribe. . . . At the same time, he divided the whole country into thirty parts: . . . ten from the city quarters, ten from the shore district, and ten from the interior. These parts he called Trittyes and assigned three of them by lot to each tribe, in such a way that each tribe would have one portion from all the main regions of the country. . . .

After these reforms the political structure became much more democratic than it had been under Solon. This development was in part also due to the fact that the Solonian laws had fallen into disuse under the tyranny until they were eventually obliterated and that Cleisthenes enacted new ones with the aim of winning the people's favor.

(479-462) By this time, then, the state had made great progress, having become gradually consolidated with the advance of democracy. After the Persian wars the Council of Areopagus again acquired strength and was again in control of the public life. It acquired this leadership, not by any formal decree, but in consequence of the fact that it had been responsible for the battle of Salamis. For when the generals did not know how to deal with the emergency and made a public proclamation saying that everybody should care for his own safety, the Council provided sufficient money to distribute eight drachmae to each man and so prevailed upon them to man the ships. For this reason the people

[1] Not an official position, but meaning only preeminent speaker and mover in the assembly, by common consensus. *Ed.*

[2] The old Four Tribes were originally based on family membership. During the forty or so years of the tyranny, many new citizens had been created outside of the old laws and customs, and one of Cleisthenes' goals was to regularize the citizenship of this recent and no doubt large addition to the population. *Ed.*

held it in high repute, and during this period the public order in
Athens was in an excellent state. . . . After this, when the Athenian state was growing in self-confidence and in the accumula-
tion of much wealth, [Aristeides] advised the Athenians to seize
the leadership and to give up their residence in the countryside to
come to live in the city. For they would all have their livelihood
there, some by participating in military expeditions, some by
doing garrison service, and still others by participating in public
affairs; . . . they followed this advice and placed themselves in
control of the empire; and from then on they got into the habit
of treating their allies, with the exception of Chios, Lesbos, and
Samos, as if they were the masters. . . .

They also made it possible for the masses to live comfortably,
as Aristeides had proposed. For out of the income derived from
the contributions made by the allies and from internal levies more
than two thousand persons were maintained. [Aristotle proceeds
to specify the numbers of jurors, councilmen, state officials, military and police]. . . . All these persons received their livelihood
from the state. . . .

For seventeen years following the Persian Wars, the political
order remained essentially the same under the supervision of
the Areopagus, although it was slowly degenerating. But as the
common people grew in strength, Ephialtes, the son of Sopho-
nides, who had a reputation for incorruptibility and loyalty to
the constitution, became leader of the people and made an attack
upon that Council [that is, the Areopagus]. First he eliminated
many of its members by bringing suits against them on the
ground of administrative misconduct. Then, in the archonship of
Conon, he deprived the Council of all those prerogatives which
it recently had acquired, and which had made it the guardian
of the state, and gave some of them to the Council of Five Hundred, some to the People, and some to the law courts.

. . . Following these events, the public order was further weakened by the efforts of popular leaders to stir up the common
people. For it so happened that at this time the better people
had no real chief, since their leader Cimon, the son of Miltiades,
was rather young and had only recently began to take an active
part in politics. . . .

(461–429) After this, when Pericles started on his career as a popular leader and first earned renown, though still a rather young man, by prosecuting Cimon on his audits as a general, the constitution became even more democratic. He took away some of the powers of the Areopagus, and, what is most important, he turned Athens' aspirations definitely toward its sea power. As a result of these changes, the masses gained still greater self-confidence and took more of the control of the state into their own hands.[3]

In the forty-ninth year after the battle of Salamis, . . . [431], the Peloponnesian War broke out. During this war the population was shut up in the city and became accustomed to being paid from public funds while on their military campaigns; and so, partly of their own will, partly without even noticing it, the common people chose to administer the state themselves.

Pericles was also the first to introduce payment for service on the law courts, a measure by which he tried to win popular favor to counteract the influence of Cimon's wealth. For Cimon, who possessed a truly regal fortune, performed the regular public services in a magnificent manner, and, in addition, supported a good many of his fellow demesmen. . . .

Pericles' resources were quite unequal to such lavish liberality. So he followed the advice of Damonides of Oea, who was generally believed to have been the instigator of most of Pericles' measures, and was later ostracized for that reason. This man had advised Pericles to "offer the people what was their own," since he was handicapped as far as his own private means were concerned; and in consequence of this, Pericles instituted pay for the judges. Some people blame him on this account and say that the law courts deteriorated, since after that it was always the common men rather than the better men who were eager to participate in drawing the lot for duty in the law courts. . . .

(429–405) As long as Pericles was the leader of the people, the state was still in a fairly good condition, but after his death every-

---

[3] Aristotle's reasoning here is that the rowers and sailors (who were paid wages) now became more important than the hoplites of the army, who were property owners and had to pay for their own equipment and support. *Ed.*

thing became much worse. For then the people first chose a leader who was not in good repute with the better people, while in the earlier period, the political leadership had always been in the hands of the latter. . . .

After the death of Pericles, Nicias, who later died in Sicily, became the leader of the aristocratic party, and Cleon, the son of Cleaenetus, the leader of the people. This man, more than anybody else, appears to have corrupted the people by his violent methods. He was the first who shouted on the public platform, who used abusive language and who spoke with his cloak girt up about him, while all the others used to speak in proper dress and manner. After this, Theramenes, the son of Hagnon, was the leader of the [aristocratic] party, and Cleophon, the owner of a lyre factory, the leader of the people. . . .

After Cleophon there was an unbroken succession of popular leaders who distinguished themselves above all by their brazenness and by their eagerness to cater to the wishes of the masses, having nothing in mind but their most immediate interests.

[Aristotle now proceeds to describe in some detail the brief oligarchic coups of the "400" in 411 and of the "30" in 404.]. . . .

This [that is, the restored democracy of 403] was the eleventh of the changes of the constitution. The first change of the original state of things occurred when Ion and his companions came to dwell with them [in the mythological period]. For it was at this time that they were grouped together in the four tribes and that the tribe-kings were first established. The second change, and the first after this which implied something of a constitutional order, was the one which happened under Theseus [in the generation before the Trojan War]. This was a slight deviation from the pure monarchy. After this came the constitution which prevailed under Draco, in which, for the first time, they drew up a code of laws [c. 620]. The third was the one under Solon, . . . from which democracy had its beginnings. The fourth was the tyranny under Pisistratus. The fifth was the constitution of Cleisthenes after the overthrow of the tyrants, a constitution more democratic than that of Solon. The sixth was the one after the Persian War, when the Council of the Areopagus had the leadership. The seventh was the one which followed this constitution;

it had been anticipated to some extent by Aristeides, but was brought to completion by Ephialtes when he deprived the Areopagus of its power. Under this constitution, the greatest mistakes were committed by the nation under the influence of the demagogues and for the sake of the domination of the sea. The eighth was the establishment of the Four Hundred. After this, the ninth was the restored democracy. The tenth was the tyranny of the Thirty and the Ten. The eleventh was the one which came into being after the return of the exiles [that is, the democrats] . . . from which date it continued to exist until it reached its present form [Aristotle is writing in c. 330], all the time adding to its grasp of arbitrary power for the people. For the people have made themselves masters of everything and administer everything through decrees of the Assembly and decisions of the law courts, in which they hold the power. For even the juridical functions of the Council have passed into the hands of the people.

8　Plutarch: Pericles—Statesman or Demagogue?

It is easy, from our perspective, to criticize Aristotle's political logic. But one should never underestimate the influence he had on subsequent writers and thinkers of the ancient world, who felt that if Aristotle had said a thing, it must be so. The imprint of his political philosophy is particularly evident in this selection from Plutarch's Life of Pericles.

Plutarch of Chaeronea was one of the most learned men of antiquity. Born in central Greece, in the middle of the first century A.D., into a world of profound peace and increasing prosperity under Roman rule, he was an eager student of the entire Greek literary heritage. Although he wrote on every subject under the sun, his best known work is a collection of biographies of famous Greeks and Romans, which he says he composed in order to direct his readers toward the virtuous life by providing examples from the past. As a Greek of wealth, property, and position, living more than five centuries after the flowering of Athenian democracy, Plutarch

*had little understanding of the vigor and intensity of public life in
the Athens of Pericles. During his own lifetime, all affairs were
handled calmly and efficiently by the officials of a benevolent yet
authoritarian Roman monarchy, and a skillful politician was one who
could worm his way into the Emperor's favor.*

*Therefore, Plutarch never had an opportunity to form an opinion
about democracy from his own experience and he was forced to
rely on the sentiments of older writers who were almost universally
hostile to the institution. Although he was a frequent resident of
Athens and admired the almost unearthly beauty of the monuments
built during Pericles' day, his judgment of the democratic regime
that built these monuments is largely unfavorable and is patently
based on the criticism of Plato and Aristotle.*

Since Thucydides describes the rule of Pericles as an aristocratical government, that went by the name of a democracy, but
was, indeed, the supremacy of a single great man, while many
others[1] say, on the contrary, that by him the common people
were first encouraged and led on to such evils as appropriations of
subject territory, allowances for attending theatres, payments for
performing public duties, and by these bad habits were, under the
influence of his public measures, changed from a sober, thrifty
people, that maintained themselves by their own labours, to lovers
of expense, intemperance, and licence, let us examine the cause
of this change by the actual matters of fact.

At the first, as has been said, when he set himself against Cimon's great authority, he did caress the people. Finding himself
come short of his competitor in wealth and money, by which
advantages the other was enabled to take care of the poor, in-
viting every day some one or other of the citizens that was in

[1] Plutarch is thinking here of Plato, *Gorgias,* and of Aristotle's *Constitution of Athens. Ed.*

SOURCE. From *Plutarch, The Lives of the Noble Grecians and Romans,*
translated by John Dryden and revised by Arthur Hugh Clough, New
York: Modern Library.

want to supper, and bestowing clothes on the aged people, and breaking down the hedges and enclosures of his grounds, that all that would might freely gather what fruit they pleased, Pericles, thus outdone in popular arts, by the advice of one Damonides of Œa, as Aristotle states, turned to the distribution of the public moneys; and in a short time having bought the people over, what with moneys allowed for shows and for service on juries, and what with other forms of pay and largess, he made use of them against the council of Areopagus of which he himself was no member, as having never been appointed by lot either chief archon, or lawgiver, or king, or captain. For from of old these offices were conferred on persons by lot, and they who had acquitted themselves duly in the discharge of them were advanced to the court of Areopagus. And so Pericles, having secured his power in interest with the populace, directed the exertions of his party against this council with such success, that most of these causes and matters which had been used to be tried there were, by the agency of Ephialtes, removed from its cognisance; Cimon, also, was banished by ostracism as a favourer of the Lacedæmonians and a hater of the people, though in wealth and noble birth he was among the first, and had won several most glorious victories over the barbarians, and had filled the city with money and spoils of war; as is recorded in the history of his life. So vast an authority had Pericles obtained among the people. . . .

Cimon, while he was admiral, ended his days in the Isle of Cyprus. And the aristocratical party, seeing that Pericles was already before this grown to be the greatest and foremost man of all the city, but nevertheless wishing there should be somebody set up against him, to blunt and turn the edge of his power, that it might not altogether prove a monarchy, put forward Thucydides of Alopece, a discreet person, and a near kinsman of Cimon's, to conduct the opposition against him; who, indeed, though less skilled in warlike affairs than Cimon was, yet was better versed in speaking and political business and keeping close guard in the city, and, engaging with Pericles on the hustings, in a short time brought the government to an equality of parties. For he would not suffer those who were called the honest and good (persons of worth and distinction) to be scattered up and down and mix themselves and be lost among the populace, as formerly, diminishing and obscuring their superiority amongst the masses; but taking them apart by themselves and uniting them in one body, by their combined weight he was able, as it were upon the balance, to make a counterpoise to the other party.

For, indeed, there was from the beginning a sort of concealed split, or seam, as it might be in a piece of iron, marking the different popular and aristocratical tendencies; but the open rivalry and contention of these two opponents made the gash deep, and severed the city into the two parties of the people and the few. And so Pericles, at that time, more than at any other, let loose the reins to the people, and made his policy subservient to their pleasure, contriving continually to have some great public show or solemnity, some banquet, or some procession or other in the town to please them, coaxing his countrymen like children with such delights and pleasures as were not, however, unedifying. Besides that every year he sent out threescore galleys, on board of which there were numbers of the citizens, who were in pay eight months, learning at the same time and practising the art of seamanship.

He sent, moreover, a thousand of them into the Chersonese as planters, to share the land among them by lot, and five hundred more into the isle of Naxos, and half that number to Andros, a thousand into Thrace to dwell among the Bisaltæ, and others into Italy, when the city Sybaris, which now was called Thurii, was to be repeopled. And this he did to ease and discharge the city of an idle, and, by reason of their idleness, a busy meddling crowd of people; and at the same time to meet the necessities and restore the fortunes of the poor townsmen, and to intimidate, also, and check their allies from attempting any change, by posting such garrisons, as it were, in the midst of them.

That which gave most pleasure and ornament to the city of Athens, and the greatest admiration and even astonishment to all strangers, and that which now is Greece's only evidence that the power she boasts of and her ancient wealth are no romance or idle story, was his construction of the public and sacred buildings. Yet this was that of all his actions in the government which his enemies most looked askance upon and cavilled at in the popular assemblies, crying out how that the commonwealth of Athens had lost its reputation and was ill-spoken of abroad for removing the common treasure of the Greeks from the isle of Delos into their own custody; and how that their fairest excuse for so doing, namely, that they took it away for fear the barbarians should seize it, and on purpose to secure it in a safe place, this Pericles had made unavailable, and how that "Greece cannot but resent it as an insufferable affront, and consider herself to be tyrannised over openly, when she sees the treasure, which was contributed by her upon a necessity for the war, wantonly lavished out by us upon our city, to gild her all over, and to adorn and set her forth, as it were some vain woman, hung round with precious stones and figures and temples, which cost a world of money."

Pericles, on the other hand, informed the people, that they were in no way obliged to give any account of those moneys to their allies, so long as they maintained their defence, and kept off the barbarians from attacking them; while in the meantime they did not so much as supply one horse or man or ship, but only found money for the service; "which money," said he, "is not theirs that give it, but theirs that receive it, if so be they perform the conditions upon which they receive it." And that it was good reason, that, now the city was sufficiently provided and stored with all things necessary for the war, they should convert the overplus of its wealth to such undertakings as would hereafter, when completed, give them eternal honour, and, for the present, while in process, freely supply all the inhabitants with plenty. With their variety of workmanship and of occasions for service, which summon all arts and trades and require all hands to be employed about them, they do actually put the whole city, in a manner, into state-pay; while at the same time she is both beautiful and maintained by herself. For as those who are of age and strength for war are provided for and maintained in the armaments abroad by their pay out of the public stock, so, it being his desire and design that the undisciplined mechanic multitude that stayed at home should not go without their share of public salaries, and yet should not have them given them for sitting still and doing nothing, to that end he thought fit to bring in among them, with the approbation of the people, these vast projects of buildings and designs of work, that would be of some continuance before they were finished, and would give employment to numerous arts, so that the part of the people that stayed at home might, no less than those that were at sea or in garrisons or on expeditions, have a fair and just occasion of receiving the benefit and having their share of the public moneys.

The materials were stone, brass, ivory, gold, ebony, cypress-wood; and the arts or trades that wrought and fashioned them were smiths and carpenters, moulders, founders and braziers, stone-cutters, dyers, goldsmiths, ivory-workers, painters, embroiderers, turners; those again that conveyed them to the town for use, merchants and mariners and ship-masters by sea, and by land, cartwrights, cattle-breeders, waggoners, rope-makers, flax-workers, shoemakers and leather-dressers, road-makers, miners. And every trade in the same nature, as a captain in an army has his particular company of soldiers under him, had its own hired company of journeymen and labourers belonging to it banded together as in array, to be as it were the instrument and body for the performance of the service. Thus, to say all in a word, the occasions and services of these public works distributed plenty through every age and condition.

As then grew the works up, no less stately in size than exquisite in form, the workmen striving to outvie the material and the design with the beauty of their workmanship, yet the most wonderful thing of all was the rapidity of their execution.

Undertakings, any one of which singly might have required, they thought, for their completion, several successions and ages of men, were every one of them accomplished in the height and prime of one man's political service. Although they say, too, that Zeuxis once, having heard Agatharchus the painter boast of despatching his work with speed and ease, replied, "I take a long time." For ease and speed in doing a thing do not give the work lasting solidity or exactness of beauty; the expenditure of time allowed to a man's pains beforehand for the production of a thing is repaid by way of interest with a vital force for the preservation when once produced. For which reason Pericles's works are especially admired, as having been made quickly, to last long. For every particular piece of his work was immediately, even at that time, for its beauty and elegance, antique; and yet in its vigour and freshness looks to this day as if it were just executed. There is a sort of bloom of newness upon those works of his, preserving them from the touch of time, as if they had some perennial spirit and underlying vitality mingled in the composition of them.

Phidias had the oversight of all the works, and was surveyor-general, though upon the various portions other great masters and workmen were employed. For Callicrates and Ictinus built the Parthenon; the chapel at Eleusis, where the mysteries were celebrated, was begun by Corœbus, who erected the pillars that stand upon the floor or pavement, and joined them to the architraves; and after his death Metagenes of Xypete added the frieze and the upper line of columns; Xenocles of Cholargus roofed or arched the lantern on top of the temple of Castor and Pollux; and the long wall, which Socrates says he himself heard Pericles propose to the people, was undertaken by Callicrates. This work Cratinus ridicules, as long in finishing—

> 'Tis long since Pericles, if words would do it,
> Talked up the wall; yet adds not one mite to it.

The Odeum, or music-room, which in its interior was full of seats and ranges of pillars, and outside had its roof made to slope and descend from one single point at the top, was constructed, we are told, in imitation of the King of Persia's Pavilion; this likewise by Pericles's order; which Cratinus again, in his comedy called the Thracian Women, made an occasion of raillery—

> So, we see here,
> Jupiter Long-pate Pericles appear,
> Since ostracism time, he's laid aside his head,
> And wears the new Odeum in its stead....

The propylæa, or entrances to the Acropolis, were finished in five years' time, Mnesicles being the principal architect. A strange accident happened in the course of building, which showed that the goddess was not averse to the work, but was aiding and co-operating to bring it to perfection. One of the artificers, the quickest and the handiest workman among them all, with a slip of his foot fell down from a great height, and lay in a miserable condition, the physicians having no hope of his recovery. When

Pericles was in distress about this, Athena appeared to him at night in a dream, and ordered a course of treatment, which he applied, and in a short time and with great ease cured the man. And upon this occasion it was that he set up a brass statue of Athena, surnamed Health, in the citadel near the altar, which they say was there before. But it was Phidias who wrought the goddess's image in gold, and he has his name inscribed on the pedestal as the workman of it; and indeed the whole work in a manner was under his charge, and he had, as we have said already, the oversight over all the artists and workmen, through Pericles's friendship for him; and this, indeed, made him much envied, and his patron shamefully slandered with stories, as if Phidias were in the habit of receiving, for Pericles's use, freeborn women that came to see the works. The comic writers of the town, when they had got hold of this story, made much of it, and bespattered him with all the ribaldry they could invent, charging him falsely with the wife of Menippus, one who was his friend and served as lieutenant under him in the wars; and with the birds kept by Pyrilampes, an acquaintance of Pericles, who, they pretended, used to give presents of peacocks to Pericles's female friends. And how can one wonder at any number of strange assertions from men whose whole lives were devoted to mockery, and who were ready at any time to sacrifice the reputation of their superiors to vulgar envy and spite, as to some evil genius, when even Stesimbrotus the Thracian has dared to lay to the charge of Pericles a monstrous and fabulous piece of criminality with his son's wife? So very difficult a matter is it to trace and find out the truth of anything by history, when, on the one hand, those who afterwards write it find long periods of time intercepting their view, and, on the other hand, the contemporary records of any actions and lives, partly through envy and ill-will, partly through favour and flattery, pervert and distort truth.

When the orators, who sided with Thucydides and his party, were at one time crying out, as their custom was, against Pericles, as one who squandered away the public money, and made havoc of the state revenues, he rose in the open assembly and put the question to the people, whether they thought that he had laid out much; and they saying, "Too much, a great deal," "Then," said he, "since it is so, let the cost not go to your account, but to mine; and let the inscription upon the buildings stand in my name." When they heard him say thus, whether it were out of a surprise to see the greatness of his spirit or out of emulation of the glory of the works, they cried aloud, bidding him to spend on, and lay out what he thought fit from the public purse, and to spare no cost, till all were finished.

At length, coming to a final contest with Thucydides which of the two should ostracise the other out of the country, and having gone through this peril, he threw his antagonist out, and broke up the confederacy that had been organised against him. So that now all schism and division being at an end, and the city brought to evenness and unity, he got all Athens and all affairs that pertained to the Athenians into his own hands, their tributes, their armies, and their galleys, the islands, the sea, and their wide-extended power, partly over other Greeks and partly over barbarians, and all that empire, which they possessed, founded and fortified upon subject nations and royal friendships and alliances.

After this he was no longer the same man he had been before, nor as tame and gentle and familiar as formerly with the populace, so as readily to yield to their pleasures and to comply with the desires of the multitude, as a steersman shifts with the winds. Quitting that loose, remiss, and, in some cases, licentious court of the popular will, he turned those soft and flowery modulations to the austerity of aristocratical and regal rule; and employing this uprightly and undeviatingly for the country's best interests, he was able generally to lead the people along, with their own wills and consents, by persuading and showing them what was to be done; and sometimes, too, urging and pressing them forward extremely against their will, he made them, whether they would or no, yield submission to what was for their advantage. In which, to say the truth, he did but like a skilful physician, who, in a complicated and chronic disease, as he sees occasion, at one while allows his patient the moderate use of such things as please him, at another while gives him keen pains and drug to work the cure. For there arising and growing up, as was natural, all manner of distempered feelings among a people which had so vast a command and dominion, he alone, as a great master, knowing how to

handle and deal fitly with each one of them, and, in an especial
manner, making that use of hopes and fears, as his two chief rud-
ders, with the one to check the career of their confidence at any
time, with the other to raise them up and cheer them when under
any discouragement, plainly showed by this, that rhetoric, or the
art of speaking, is, in Plato's language, the government of the souls
of men, and that her chief business is to address the affections and
passions, which are as it were the strings and keys to the soul, and
require a skilful and careful touch to be played on as they should
be. The source of this predominance was not barely his power of
language, but, as Thucydides assures us, the reputation of his life,
and the confidence felt in his character; his manifest freedom from
every kind of corruption, and superiority to all considerations of
money. Notwithstanding he had made the city of Athens, which
was great of itself, as great and rich as can be imagined, and
though he were himself in power and interest more than equal
to many kings and absolute rulers, who some of them also be-
queathed by will their power to their children, he, for his part,
did not make the patrimony his father left him greater than it was
by one drachma.

9   *Arnold Toynbee: A Moralist Condemns Imperialism*

*Perhaps no historian in the world is so well known or so hotly
discussed as the English scholar, Arnold Toynbee. Born in 1889,
Toynbee was educated at Oxford. Both his University training and
his first teaching post were in Ancient History, but his enormous
learning soon led him to escape the boundaries of any one narrow
period and to take the whole of human history as his province. His
massive, ten volume* Study of History, *published between 1934 and
1954, reveals his belief in the continuity of human experience, the
recurrence of various types of challenge and response, and the influence of spiritual forces in shaping history.*

Toynbee's choice of the broad canvas on which to depict the story of mankind has often inspired him to make sweeping moral judgments about whole civilizations. In this passage from a shorter study of Graeco-Roman civilization, he condemns the growth of the Athenian empire for its effect on Athenian moral fiber. In general, I disagree strongly both with Toynbee's evaluation of the evidence, and with his tendency to tell us how history ought to have come out. For instance, the historian seems to follow Plutarch in believing (mistakenly, one should add) that the great temples of Athens were merely public works projects, created to avoid unemployment.

But a collection such as this should include the provocative and the controversial, and no student of historical method can deny that both these qualities are more than adequately represented in the following selection.

The confederacy that had been established in 478 B.C., for mutual defence, between Athens and the Hellenic states liberated from Persian rule had had a good start. The first business on the new allies' agenda had been to settle the quotas that each state should contribute to the common cause and the form which the contributions should take. The negotiation of this business had been entrusted to the Athenian statesman Aristeides, and he had carried out his task with a fair-mindedness that had shone by contrast with the recent misconduct of the Spartan regent Pausanias. Two previous Persian acts of state had given Aristeides foundations to build on. After the suppression of the Asian Hellenic states, revolt in 494 B.C., Darius I's brother, Artaphrenes, had reassessed their tribute to the Persian Government and had also put pressure on them to make commercial treaties with one another in order that disputes over matters of business between citizens of different states might be settled by action at law in place of the former barbarous custom of distraining by force of arms on any property within reach belonging to citizens of the

SOURCE. Arnold Toynbee, *Hellenism*, New York: Oxford University Press, 1959, pp. 105–110. Reprinted by permission of Oxford University Press.

other party's country. Here was a ready-made basis for a voluntary confederation between Athens and the states that she had
now liberated from Persian rule. The principal charge on the
finances of the new confederacy would be the maintenance of a
common navy; and it was obvious that the lion's share of the
ships and crews would continue to be furnished by Athens, since
she already had a great fleet in being. The larger and wealthier
of the other states could also furnish naval squadrons. But the
cost of building, fitting out, and maintaining even a single war-
ship of the new and more expensive type put into commission by
the Athenians since 482 B.C. was beyond the means of many, perhaps of most, of the confederate states. So, for the sake of both
fairness and efficiency, it was agreed that any state, in lieu of
furnishing a ship or ships, might pay an annual contribution in
money, to be assessed by Aristeides, into a federal treasury that
was to be set up on the holy island of Delos. This revenue was
to be spent on subsidizing the Athenian navy, since Athens was
furnishing the greater part of the ships.

The These arrangements had been freely accepted with the best
intentions on all sides. Aristeides' assessment had earned him the
title of "the Just." But the new confederacy had soon run into
trouble. When states members—especially those which, like the
Euboean states and Naxos and Thasos, were now no longer the
Persian Empire's immediate neighbours—had tried to secede,
Athens had treated secession as high treason; had subdued the
secessionists by force of arms; and, to ensure that they should
not be able to try again, had deprived them of their warships and
had imposed heavy annual money contributions on them. In 454 B.C.
the confederacy's treasury had been moved from Delos to Athens
(nominally on the ground that Delos was exposed to the danger
of a Persian attack after the Athenian naval disaster in Egypt).
By the time when Athens made peace with Persia in 450/49 B.C.
there were only seven states left in the confederacy, apart from
Athens herself, that were still furnishing ships: namely Samos,
Chios, and the five states on the island of Lesbos. All the rest were
now paying tribute.

The states on the west coast of the Asian mainland and on the
adjoining islands had had . . . to pay a high economic price for their

political liberation. This had cut them off from their commercial hinterland in the interior of the Persian Empire by the interposition of a military front. The Atheno-Persian peace treaty of 450/49 B.C. now placed them militarily at the mercy of both contracting parties by providing that their fortifications should be dismantled. No provision seems to have been made for the resumption of their lost trade with their Persian hinterland.[1] But, now that the war was over, all the money-contributing states of the Delian confederacy expected at any rate to be relieved of this financial burden.

This reasonable expectation on their part produced an internal political crisis in Athens. One effect of the constitution of the confederacy of Delos, as it had operated in the course of thirty years, had been to make the earning of wages as oarsmen for the Athenian navy one of the main sources of livelihood for the landless urban majority of the population of Attica; and these wages had been paid out of the fund provided by the contributions of Athens' allies. There would be mass unemployment at Athens if the financial means could not continue to be found for providing the same wages for the same number of Athenian citizens in some alternative occupation to naval service. Could new work be found for which wages could be paid to the discharged Athenian naval crews? And, since Athens' own national budget would not run to bearing this formidable new charge permanently, would it be right to finance it out of contributions levied from the allies in peace-time? Pericles was a gentlemanly and cultivated politician (he was an aristocrat on his mother's side), and he owed his hold over the Athenian people to their appreciation of his superior qualities. But, in a democracy such as Athens now was, his leadership would not survive the calamity of mass unemployment. Pericles therefore took the line that the allies' monetary contributions to the common treasury were in the nature of annual premiums paid to Athens for insurance against the risk of a Persian re-conquest; and that, so long as Athens continued,

---

[1] Toynbee's assumption of state control of trade is an anachronism. There is evidence to show that trade between Ionia and areas under Persian control went on as usual, even when a state of war officially existed. *Ed.*

whether by naval warfare or by treaty, to keep the Persian Empire's hands off its former Hellenic subjects, Athens was entitled to spend the money as she might think best. Pericles proposed that it should now be spent on rebuilding Hellenic temples destroyed by the Persian aggressors in 480–479 B.C.—i.e., in effect, the temples on the citadel of Athens. Aristeides' role was taken up in the Athenian national assembly by Thucydides son of Melesias; but, when the assembly had to decide between doing justice to the allies and providing for the continuance of remunerative public employment for its own members, self-interest prevailed. The consequences of this decision, taken in 443 B.C., were the creation of consummate Athenian works of art and the breakdown, decline, and fall of the Hellenic civilization of which these works were such outstanding products and monuments.

Another remunerative public employment at Athens was that of serving as jurymen (the juries were large and, for the trial of certain cases, were coextensive with the whole body of citizens entitled to vote in the assembly; and, on Pericles' initiative, they were paid for their services from 451–450 B.C. onwards). Since 478 B.C., Athens had been capturing more and more of the trade of the Hellenic World from her own Asian Hellenic allies and from the Isthmian allies of Sparta. This meant that an increasing proportion of actions at law between citizens of different states under bilateral commercial treaties were coming to be tried in Athenian courts. Athens now abused her power over her allies by compelling them to bring suits for trial to Athens even when the case was not a commercial one and even when the defendant was not an Athenian citizen. From the Athenian point of view this policy had two advantages: the economic one of bringing more pay into Athenian jurymen's pockets and the political one of giving opportunities for penalizing the well-to-do citizens of allied states, who were apt to be anti-Athenian because the tribute came out of their pockets, and for favouring the masses, who were apt to be loyal to Athens because they had nothing to lose and much to gain by their country's alliance with the Athenian democracy.

By 451–450 B.C. the Athenian franchise had become so valuable that in that year, at Pericles' instance, the national assembly passed a law restricting the franchise to men who could prove that both their parents were Athenian citizens. The consequent purge of the citizen body was carried out harshly five years later.

Thus, within thirty years, the Athenian democracy had gone the way of its Spartiate predecessor. It had become a parasitic military 'ascendancy' with its own helots (the tribute-paying "allies") and perioeci (the allies who were still privileged to contribute naval squadrons). Cleon, Pericles' ungentlemanly but unhypocritical successor in the political leadership of the Athenian people during the first bout of the second Atheno-Peloponnesian war, told his countrymen, with brutal frankness, that Athens had become a 'dictator state,' and that her only hope of maintaining her now tyrannous rule lay in a policy of 'frightfulness.'

This degeneration of the confederacy of Delos into an Athenian empire was a tragedy. For, in this age, closer political union was, in itself, just what the Hellenic World needed, not only for defence against the Persian Empire but also, as we have seen, for providing the political framework for the already accomplished fact of economic interdependence. If the Athenians had resisted the temptation to abuse their trust, as the leading power in the confederacy, for their own narrow national advantage, the economic tide making for closer political union would probably have kept the confederacy of Delos in existence on a voluntary footing; and this might have led on, in time, to some kind of voluntary political unification of the Hellenic World as a whole. The course taken, at this critical time, by Athenian policy under Pericles' leadership led to a renewal of fratricidal warfare, the breakdown of the Hellenic civilization, and the tardy political unification of the Hellenic World by overwhelming Roman force.

10 *André Bonnard: A Humanist Interprets Political Comedy*

Because our sources for Athenian history are so limited, scholars often feel themselves compelled to use all available types of information. For the period of the Peloponnesian War, one inevitably turns to that great free spirit of comic genius, the playwright Aristophanes, whose comedies were as topical as a political cartoon, and as subtle as a punch in the nose.

The first aim of Aristophanes was to be funny. Like all the other comic poets of Athens, he took current situations and famous local figures and, by drawing caricatures extreme to the point of fantasy, attempted to reduce his audience to helpless laughter. But scholars have never been able to agree how much of Aristophanes is simple caricature, and how much is real social and political criticism (very much the same sort of disagreement goes on today, every day of the week, over Pogo *or* Li'l Abner*).*

Aristophanes' plays are often cruel parodies—of the gross and corrupt Cleon, of woolgathering sophists, of country bumpkins, and of the Athenian Demos itself. In this selection, the French scholar André Bonnard goes a step further and sees in the plays a savage indictment of the direction Athenian society was taking at the end of the fifth century B.C.

Once again, I am in strenuous disagreement with the interpretation encountered here, but I include the selection in the hope that readers will be encouraged to read Aristophanes themselves and to make up their own minds.

One object of Pericles' imperial policy—whether a primary or secondary object, I do not know—was to provide a means of livelihood for the mass of the people. His policy succeeded in this

SOURCE. From *Greek Civilization from the Antigone to Socrates*. A. Lytton Sells, tr., London: Allen and Unwin, 1959, pp. 203–210.

partly by the grant of pay to the armies, partly by the construction of great public buildings which provided work for numerous classes of craftsmen, work which, when it came to the point, was paid for by the tribute of the allies and the subject-states.

But an imperialist policy led to an imperialist war. The empire quickly became, for Athens herself, a terrible "tyranny" (Thucydides puts the word into the mouth of Pericles). It became something like a system of cog-wheels or gears in which Athens herself was caught and finally crushed. Rebellion succeeded rebellion. Sparta was watching for her opportunity. Meanwhile the tribute of the allies remained indispensable for feeding and amusing the sovereign people. To escape from the cogs one would have had first to win the war. Athens lost it and was ruined. . . .

Plato's Socrates scarcely exaggerates when he accuses Pericles of having made the Athenians "idle, base, talkative and greedy." Pericles was in fact responsible for the formation of that body of indolent citizens who expected the State to feed and amuse them. The State by turns paid out their wages, or paid them for attending the theatre, or sent them to get killed on the battlefields of the Peloponnese or of Thrace. But they would not for long be willing even to defend the Athens that was supporting them. Soon there was to be no more citizen-army. To maintain the wars which were to provide their "dividends" the citizen-shareholders of Athenian democracy were to demand the engagement of mercenary troops. Civic pride did not long survive the achievement of those democratic institutions which had been so dearly bought but which seemed to die for lack of progress.

These institutions indeed remained intact, but during the fifty years of the golden age they became fixed in a dangerous immobility. It seemed as though there no longer existed a militant class to defend and improve them. The class which had produced them had fallen into a strange inertia. It was no longer a class of producers but much rather of men who exploited those who were producing. These were the metics (citizens of other states or subjects of barbarian kingdoms, men resident in Athens), the allies and especially the slaves. A drastic divorce had taken place between the beneficiaries of the régime and those who produced for it.

This exploitation of the democracy and the empire went on in the midst of a frightful muddle, of which Aristophanes—whom one should re-read, not for the pleasure of the comedy but for the image of the people—is the surest and most clear-sighted witness. Even if he on occasion idealizes certain of his characters, the peasants for example, or if, as happens more often, he caricatures and rends them too harshly—the politicians, philosophers and judges—one thing is certain about his satire and that is that he is always attacking real faults.

If we take up the *Knights* or the *Wasps* we shall discover, behind the comic fiction, an authentic image of the new masters of the people, the successors of Pericles, and an image of the people itself, with which these demagogues corresponded.

Here is the Cleon of the *Knights*, a greedy and flattering orator. To flatter the people in order to assure one's own power and to use that power to fill one's pockets! How far we have suddenly become removed from the Pericles of Thucydides, "entirely incorruptible," a man who spoke to the assembled people only "to give them the best advice." Flattery had now become a means of government with respect to that plebeian mass whom war had rendered idle and whose demands already give a foretaste of the "panem et circenses" of the Roman populace. Listen to the demagogue addressing the Sovereign People (I quote or summarize passages from various parts of the play): "Demus, I love thee, I am enamoured of thee."

> That over all Hellas our Demus may rule, for do not the oracles say,
> He will surely his verdicts in Arcady give, receiving five obols a day . . . ?
> Wait till you've heard my oracles, I pray. . . .
> Nay mine foretell that over all the land
> Thyself shalt rule, with roses garlanded . . .
> O Demus dear, be idle all the day,
> And I'll provide you free to swill, a foaming bowl—of pay!

"Take a bath, gorge and stuff yourself. . . . Here's some jugged hare, here are some presents. . . . Here's my own tunic. . . . Here's

a plateful of wages to gobble up, and no need to work for them."
Thus, right through the play, Cleon tirelessly and methodically
proposes to corrupt the people with flattery, with the bait of
pleasures and money and idleness. "I know the people," he says,
"I know how one lays bait for it, . . . and that is why it belongs
to me."

Here now is the same Cleon, flattery laid aside and as he really
is. He unleashes himself like a typhoon ("the most violent of all
citizens," say Thucydides), with a tempest of threats. Those who
are truly serving the people, he denounces and causes to be punished. Why? So that he can be paid and bought off. He is a black-
mailer. In everything and everywhere "he alights upon the
flowers of venality." He demands, extorts, confiscates. Those
among the rich who are his enemies, he causes to be registered
for taxation.

> Chorus. *And you squeeze the audit-passers, squeezing*
> *them like figs, to try*
> *Which is ripe, and which is ripening, which is*
> *very crude and dry....*
>
> Sausage-Seller. *I denounce this juggling fellow; at the Hall,*
> *from day to day,*
> *In he runs with empty belly, with a full one hies*
> *away....*
>
> Chorus. *Ruffian, who has deafened Athens with thine*
> *everlasting din,*
> *Watching from the rocks the tribute, tunny-*
> *fashion, shoaling in.*

"He gobbles up the islands as a dog licks up what is on the plate";
and offering Demus, the Sovereign People, only a small slice of
nothing at all, he keeps "the huge share of the cake" for himself.
Our metaphors have not changed.

He is a greedy and thieving flatterer and boasts of it. "I boast
of my thefts," he tells his rival. "You don't . . . when I'm caught
red-handed, I perjure myself."

Secondary features add further touches to the portrait. Cleon is a coward (as in Thucydides), a coarse and uncultured "black-guard," obscene and debauched. Not to speak of his repulsive physique. He is a ginger-haired man who stinks like a seal, he is a baboon. I omit other features.

Such was the most colourful of Pericles' successors. And why? Because the people had the masters it deserved. But let us first glance at that satire on the Athenian legal system, that picture of a people with a mania for chicanery and litigation—the famous *Wasps*, from which Racine was to draw his amusing comedy of *Les Plaideurs*.

The Wasps clearly brings out the necessity of multiplying the number of lawsuits in order to provide a livelihood for the population of judges; for otherwise it would mean starvation for this multitude who have lost any possibility of work and any taste for it.

> Boy. *Father, if the Archon say*
> *That the Court won't sit today,*
> *Tell me truly, father mine,*
> *Have we wherewithal to dine?*

Here then we have a class of people who can only live, and live pretty miserably, unless they have other resources, on a multitude of lawsuits. Those lawsuits were occasioned by denunciations. There was a tacit but perfectly conscious agreement between the demagogues and the judges. In order to provide for this proletariat of legal officials, the politicians brought innumerable lawsuits against individuals, or arranged for them so to be brought. A system of delation reigned in the city. And the people, who were grateful to the point of servility to those who fed them, supported in the Assembly the policy of the men who supplied them with cases to judge. By this kind of pact each party became enslaved to the other. Aristophanes denounces the pact of mutual enslavement. The judge Philocleon, who is the principal character in the play, rightly boasts of having domesticated the demagogues:

> *Yea, Cleon the Bawler and Brawler himself, at us, and us only,*
> *to nibble forbears,*

*And sweeps off the flies that annoy us, and still with a vigilant
hand for our dignity cares.*

*Yet Theorus, a statesman as noble and grand as lordly Euphe-
mius, runs at our call,*

*And whips out a sponge from his bottle, and stoops, to black
and to polish the shoes of us all.*

But Bdelycleon (that is, the man who feels sick at the name of
Cleon) points out to his father Philocleon, and with quite as much
reason, that his father is a slave without suspecting it. The demagogues, who were much more cunning than the officials, got the
major share of the profits. [The son points out that whereas the
annual revenue is about two thousand talents a year, the judges
receive only one hundred and fifty—less than a tenth. Trans-
lator.]

> Philocleon. . . . *And what becomes of all the rest of the revenue
> pray?*
> Bdelycleon. *Why, bless you, it goes to the pockets of those,*
> *"To the rabble of Athens I'll ever be true,*
> *I'll always battle away for the mob." O father my
> father, 'tis owing to you:*
> *By such small phrases as these cajoled, you lift
> them over yourselves to reign.*
> *And then, believe me, they soon contrive some
> fifty talents in bribes to gain,*
> *Extorting them out of the subject states, by hostile
> menace and angry frown.*

The politicians however religiously observed that clause of the
pact which obliged them to supply the judges with their daily
ration of lawsuits—and this for the misfortune of the country.
They made use of the sycophants, which was the name given to
the professional accusers and blackmailers; unless they preferred
themselves to exercise this most profitable of trades. The sycophants were the worst parasites of Athenian democracy, and
Aristophanes' comedies are full of them. Delation was rampant
in Athens during the Peloponnesian war. Now because the judge

had to draw his daily wage and because the quarrels of factions
were envenomed in an atmosphere of approaching defeat, Athens
was wholly poisoned by this dreadful gangrene.

We know that if this plague could develop to such propor-
tions, it was partly owing to a serious defect in the judicial system. There was no public ministry or chamber for finding a true
bill of indictment. The state did not prosecute: only the person
allegedly injured had the right to do that. Hence, if the question
arose of impeaching an act injurious to the public interest, any
citizen whosoever, as part of the community, could be the plain-
tiff and denounce the act. Hence also that swarm of accusers, especially politicians, certain of pleasing the people by bringing as
many actions as possible concerning state security. They denounced people in season and out of season. They denounced the
allied cities so as to increase the amount of their tribute. They
denounced the rich in order to confiscate their goods. They
accused people of plotting with the aliens; they accused officials
of corruption and embezzlement; they accused their fellow-
citizens of attempting to set up a tyranny, and of many other
conspiracies. Athens was living in an atmosphere of terror and
insecurity, of which we hear echoes in Thucydides as well as in
Aristophanes.

Comedy of course chose extreme cases or sometimes invented
humorous accusations. It was enough to be too elegant, to wear
a fringed cloak and a well-trimmed beard to draw on oneself
the accusation of being an enemy of the people, an aristocrat, a
monarchist. Bdelycleon points out that

> *Everywhere the name of Tyrant, now for fifty years unknown,*
> *Is than cheap salt-fish at Athens commoner and cheaper grown.*
> *Everywhere about the market it is bandied to and fro:*
> *If you wish a bass to purchase, and without a pilchard go,*
> *Straight the man who sells the pilchards grumbles from his stall*
>   *hard by,*
> *"Here is plainly one that caters with a view to Tyranny."*
> *If a leek, besides, you order, relish for your sprats perchance,*

Says the potherb-girl directly, eyeing you with looks askance,
"Leeks indeed! and leeks I prithee! what, with Tyranny in view!

The picture Aristophanes has painted of the Athenian people
and its masters is cruelly comical and borders on the grim. The
playwright has but recently been regarded as an enemy of democracy. This is an error. He was the best friend the Athenian
people had, a friend who loved his countrymen well enough to
tell them home truths. The picture is so true even in its exag-
gerations that this very darkening of the colours reveals in an
almost prophetic fashion what Athenian democracy was to become towards the middle of the fourth century.

In the time of Solon a great hope had arisen, a hope that too
soon proved abortive: a social class had been formed in Attica,
a producing class composed largely of small peasants. The city-
artisans had joined it and, engaged in the production of material
and cultural wealth, they had together exercised a revolutionary
activity productive of new institutions.

War first, then the formation of the Athenian empire and
finally its exploitation, exhausted their productive capacity and
destroyed the solid bonds which united them in participating in
the achievement of a great piece of work. This work was in fact
disappearing. Athens no longer contained a class of citizens with
equal rights and acting together in the possession of rights which
were the outcome of their work. There was now only an
agglomeration of individuals whose sole bond was soon to be poverty and hatred for a few men who were exploiting them. Confined within the city walls and doomed to idleness, the only thing
they had in common was the sharing out of wealth acquired at
the expense of an empire that was about to crumble away. They
were magistrates, officials and judges by the thousand. In order
to get their wages we know that many of them registered simultaneously in several sections of the Popular Tribunal so that after
judging one case they could immediately go and draw wages for
judging in the other sections. Their rather meagre pay was supplemented on occasion by distribution in money and kind. But,

as we see in the *Wasps*, they lamented at receiving only a very mean share of the tribute from the allies, the greater part being absorbed by military expenditure or disappearing into the pockets of the demagogues. Thus the whole economy by which they were living was illusory. The tribute from the allies and especially slave-labour were the only things that gave it a concrete existence.

11   *Thucydides: Pericles Delivers His Funeral Oration*

"In this history I have made use of set speeches some of which were delivered just before and others during the war. I have found it difficult to remember the precise words used in the speeches which I listened to myself and my various informants have experienced the same difficulty; so my method has been, while keeping as closely as possible to the general sense of the words that were actually used, to make the speakers say what, in my opinion, was called for by each situation."

Thus Thucydides describes his method of reproducing the oratory of the Peloponnesian War, and most critics today are more or less content to take his remarks at face value, believing that the content and the order of the topics brought up in Pericles' Funeral Oration have been preserved by Thucydides, but that the actual wording is the historian's own.

Thucydides was born about 470. He was, therefore, a mature man when the war started and was intimately acquainted with both the events and the personalites of Athens during the first few years of the conflict. But in 424, as a general operating in the northern Aegean, he was unfortunate enough to lose part of the area under his jurisdiction to the brilliant Spartan commander Brasidas, and the Athenian people condemned him to exile that lasted until the end of the war twenty years later. During this period he wrote his History, *remaining remarkably dispassionate and describing the successes and failures of both sides with neither elation nor rancor.*

Perhaps no part of Thucydides' work is so much read as this noble and moving speech, delivered by Pericles in honor of the war dead after the action of the first year of the war had been brought to a close by winter.

In the same winter the Athenians, following their annual custom, gave a public funeral for those who had been the first to die in the war. These funerals are held in the following way: two days before the ceremony the bones of the fallen are brought and put in a tent which has been erected, and people make whatever offerings they wish to their own dead. Then there is a funeral procession in which coffins of cypress wood are carried on wagons. There is one coffin for each tribe, which contains the bones of members of that tribe. One empty bier is decorated and carried in the procession: this is for the missing, whose bodies could not be recovered. Everyone who wishes to, both citizens and foreigners, can join in the procession, and the women who are related to the dead are there to make their laments at the tomb. The bones are laid in the public burial-place, which is in the most beautiful quarter outside the city walls. Here the Athenians always bury those who have fallen in war. The only exception is those who died at Marathon, who, because their achievement was considered absolutely outstanding, were buried on the battlefield itself.

When the bones have been laid in the earth, a man chosen by the city for his intellectual gifts and for his general reputation makes an appropriate speech in praise of the dead, and after the speech all depart. This is the procedure at these burials, and all through the war, when the time came to do so, the Athenians followed this ancient custom. Now, at the burial of those who were the first to fall in the war Pericles, the son of Xanthippus, was chosen to make the speech. When the moment arrived, he came forward from the tomb and, standing on a high platform, so that he might be heard by as many people as possible in the crowd, he spoke as follows:

SOURCE. Thucydides, *The Peloponnesian War*, Rex Warner, tr., London: Penguin Books Ltd., 1954, pp. 34–46. Copyright 1954. Reprinted by permission of The Bodley Head.

"Many of those who have spoken here in the past have praised the institution of this speech at the close of our ceremony. It seemed to them a mark of honour to our soldiers who have fallen in war that a speech should be made over them. I do not agree. These men have shown themselves valiant in action, and it would be enough, I think, for their glories to be proclaimed in action, as you have just seen it done at this funeral organized by the state. Our belief in the courage and manliness of so many should not be hazarded on the goodness or badness of one man's speech. Then it is not easy to speak with a proper sense of balance, when a man's listeners find it difficult to believe in the truth of what one is saying. The man who knows the facts and loves the dead may well think that an oration tells less than what he knows and what he would like to hear: others who do not know so much may feel envy for the dead, and think the orator over-praises them when he speaks of exploits that are beyond their own capacities. Praise of other people is tolerable only up to a certain point, the point where one still believes that one could do oneself some of the things one is hearing about. Once you get beyond this point, you will find people becoming jealous and incredulous. However, the fact is that this institution was set up and approved by our forefathers, and it is my duty to follow the tradition and do my best to meet the wishes and the expectations of every one of you.

"I shall begin by speaking about our ancestors, since it is only right and proper on such an occasion to pay them the honour of recalling what they did. In this land of ours there have always been the same people living from generation to generation up till now, and they, by their courage and their virtues, have handed it on to us, a free country. They certainly deserve our praise. Even more so do our fathers deserve it. For to the inheritance they had received they added all the empire we have now, and it was not without blood and toil that they handed it down to us of the present generation. And then we ourselves, assembled here to-day, who are mostly in the prime of life, have, in most directions, added to the power of our empire and have organized our State in such a way that it is perfectly well able to look after itself both in peace and in war.

"I have no wish to make a long speech on subjects familiar to you all: so I shall say nothing about the warlike deeds by which we acquired our power or the battles in which we or our fathers gallantly resisted our enemies, Greek or foreign. What I want to do is, in the first place, to discuss the spirit in which we faced our trials and also our constitution and the way of life which has made us great. After that I shall speak in praise of the dead, believing that this kind of speech is not inappropriate to the present occasion, and that this whole assembly, of citizens and foreigners, may listen to it with advantage.

"Let me say that our system of government does not copy the institutions of our neighbours. It is more the case of our being a model to others, than of our imitating anyone else. Our constitution is called a democracy because power is in the hands not of a minority but of the whole people. When it is a question of settling private disputes, everyone is equal before the law; when it is a question of putting one person before another in positions of public responsibility, what counts is not membership of a particular class, but the actual ability which the man possesses. No one, so long as he has it in him to be of service to the state, is kept in political obscurity because of poverty. And, just as our political life is free and open, so is our day-to-day life in our relations with each other. We do not get into a state with our next-door neighbour if he enjoys himself in his own way, nor do we give him the kind of black looks which, though they do no real harm, still do hurt people's feelings. We are free and tolerant in our private lives; but in public affairs we keep to the law. This is because it commands our deep respect.

"We give our obedience to those whom we put in positions of authority, and we obey the laws themselves, especially those which are for the protection of the oppressed, and those unwritten laws which it is an acknowledged shame to break.

"And here is another point. When our work is over, we are in a position to enjoy all kinds of recreation for our spirits. There are various kinds of contests and sacrifices regularly throughout the year; in our own homes we find a beauty and a good taste which delight us every day and which drive away our cares. Then

the greatness of our city brings it about that all the good things
from all over the world flow in to us, so that to us it seems just
as natural to enjoy foreign goods as our own local products.

"Then there is a great difference between us and our opponents,
in our attitude towards military security. Here are some examples:
Our city is open to the world, and we have no periodical deporta-
tions in order to prevent people observing or finding out secrets
which might be of military advantage to the enemy. This is because we rely, not on secret weapons, but on our own real courage
and loyalty. There is a difference, too, in our educational systems.
The Spartans, from their earliest boyhood, are submitted to the
most laborious training in courage; we pass our lives without all
these restrictions, and yet are just as ready to face the same dangers as they are. Here is a proof of this: When the Spartans invade
our land, they do not come by themselves, but bring all their
allies with them; whereas we, when we launch an attack abroad,
do the job by ourselves, and, though fighting on foreign soil, do
not often fail to defeat opponents who are fighting for their own
hearths and homes. As a matter of fact none of our enemies has
ever yet been confronted with our total strength, because we
have to divide our attention between our navy and the many
missions on which our troops are sent on land. Yet, if our enemies
engage a detachment of our forces and defeat it, they give themselves credit for having thrown back our entire army; or, if they
lose, they claim that they were beaten by us in full strength. There
are certain advantages, I think, in our way of meeting danger
voluntarily, with an easy mind, instead of with a laborious training, with natural rather than with state-induced courage. We do
not have to spend our time practising to meet sufferings which
are still in the future; and when they are actually upon us we
show ourselves just as brave as these others who are always in
strict training. This is one point in which, I think, our city deserves to be admired. There are also others:

"Our love of what is beautiful does not lead to extravagance;
our love of the things of the mind does not make us soft. We
regard wealth as something to be properly used, rather than as
something to boast about. As for poverty, no one need be ashamed
to admit it: the real shame is in not taking practical measures to

escape from it. Here each individual is interested not only in his own affairs but in the affairs of the state as well: even those who are mostly occupied with their own business are extremely well-informed on general politics—this is a peculiarity of ours: we do not say that a man who takes no interest in politics is a man who minds his own business; we say that he has no business here at all. We Athenians, in our own persons, take our decisions on policy or submit them to proper discussions: for we do not think that there is an incompatibility between words and deeds; the worst thing is to rush into action before the consequences have been properly debated. And this is another point where we differ from other people. We are capable at the same time of taking risks and of estimating them beforehand. Others are brave out of ignorance; and, when they stop to think, they begin to fear. But the man who can most truly be accounted brave is he who best knows the meaning of what is sweet in life and of what is terrible, and then goes out undeterred to meet what is to come.

"Again, in questions of general good feeling there is a great contrast between us and most other people. We make friends by doing good to others, not by receiving good from them. This makes our friendship all the more reliable, since we want to keep alive the gratitude of those who are in our debt by showing continued goodwill to them: whereas the feelings of one who owes us something lack the same enthusiasm, since he knows that, when he repays our kindness, it will be more like paying back a debt than giving something spontaneously. We are unique in this. When we do kindnesses to others, we do not do them out of any calculations of profit or loss: we do them without afterthought, relying on our free liberality. Taking everything together then, I declare that our city is an education to Greece, and I declare that in my opinion each single one of our citizens, in all the manifold aspects of life, is able to show himself the rightful lord and owner of his own person, and do this, moreover, with exceptional grace and exceptional versatility. And to show that this is no empty boasting for the present occasion, but real tangible fact, you have only to consider the power which our city possesses and which has been won by those very qualities which I have mentioned. Athens, alone of the states we know, comes to her testing time in a greatness that surpasses what was imagined of her. In her case, and in her case alone, no invading enemy is ashamed at being defeated, and no subject can complain of being governed by people unfit for their responsibilities. Mighty indeed are the marks and monuments of our empire which we have left. Future ages will wonder at us, as the present age wonders at us now. We do not need the praises of a Homer, or of anyone else whose words may delight us for the moment, but whose estimation of facts will fall short of what is really true. For our adventurous spirit has forced an entry into every sea and into every land; and everywhere we have left behind us everlasting memorials of good done to our friends or suffering inflicted on our enemies.

"This, then, is the kind of city for which these men, who could not bear the thought of losing her, nobly fought and nobly died. It is only natural that every one of us who survive them should be willing to undergo hardships in her service. And it was for this reason that I have spoken at such length about our city, because I wanted to make it clear that for us there is more at stake than there is for others who lack our advantages; also I wanted my words of praise for the dead to be set in the bright light of evidence. And now the most important of these words has been spoken. I have sung the praises of our city; but it was the courage and gallantry of these men, and of people like them, which made her splendid. Nor would you find it true in the case of many of the Greeks, as it is true of them, that no words can do more than justice to their deeds.

"To me it seems that the consummation which has overtaken these men shows us the meaning of manliness in its first revelation and in its final proof. Some of them, no doubt, had their faults; but what we ought to remember first is their gallant conduct against the enemy in defence of their native land. They have blotted out evil with good, and done more service to the commonwealth than they ever did harm in their private lives. No one of these men weakened because he wanted to go on enjoying his wealth: no one put off the awful day in the hope that he might live to escape his poverty and grow rich. More to be desired than such things, they chose to check the enemy's pride. This, to them, was a risk most glorious, and they accepted it, willing to strike down the enemy and relinquish everything else. As for success or failure, they left that in the doubtful hands of Hope, and when the reality of battle was before their faces, they put their trust in their own selves. In the fighting, they thought it more honourable to stand their ground and suffer death than to give in and save their lives. So they fled from the reproaches of men, abiding with life and limb the brunt of battle; and, in a small moment of time, the climax of their lives, a culmination of glory, not of fear, were swept away from us.

"So and such they were, these men—worthy of their city. We who remain behind may hope to be spared their fate, but must resolve to keep the same daring spirit against the foe. It is not simply a question of estimating the advantages in theory. I could tell you a long story (and you know it as well as I do) about what is to be gained by beating the enemy back. What I would prefer is that you should fix your eyes every day on the greatness of Athens as she really is, and should fall in love with her. When you realize her greatness, then reflect that what made her great was men with a spirit of adventure, men who knew their duty, men who were ashamed to fall below a certain standard. If they ever failed in an enterprise, they made up their minds that at any rate the city should not find their courage lacking to her, and they gave to her the best contribution that they could. They gave her their lives, to her and to all of us, and for their own selves they won praises that never grow old, the most splendid of sepulchres —not the sepulchre in which their bodies are laid, but where their glory remains eternal in men's minds, always there on the right occasion to stir others to speech or to action. For famous men have the whole earth as their memorial: it is not only the inscriptions on their graves in their own country that mark them out; no, in foreign lands also, not in any visible form but in people's hearts, their memory abides and grows. It is for you to try to be like them. Make up your minds that happiness depends on being free, and freedom depends on being courageous. Let there be no relaxation in face of the perils of the war. The people who have most excuse for despising death are not the wretched and unfortunate, who have no hope of doing well for themselves, but those who run the risk of a complete reversal in their lives, and who would feel the difference most intensely, if things went wrong for them. Any intelligent man would find a humiliation caused by his own slackness more painful to bear than death, when death comes to him unperceived, in battle, and in the confidence of his patriotism.

"For these reasons I shall not commiserate with those parents of the dead, who are present here. Instead I shall try to comfort them. They are well aware that they have grown up in a world where there are many changes and chances. But this is good fortune—for men to end their lives with honour, as these have done, and for you honourably to lament them: their life was set to a measure where death and happiness went hand in hand. I know that it is difficult to convince you of this. When you see other people happy you will often be reminded of what used to make you happy too. One does not feel sad at not having some good thing which is outside one's experience: real grief is felt at the loss of something which one is used to. All the same, those of you who are of the right age must bear up and take comfort in the thought of having more children. In your own homes these new children will prevent you from brooding over those who are no more, and they will be a help to the city, too, both in filling the empty places, and in assuring her security. For it is impossible for a man to put forward fair and honest views about our affairs if he has not, like everyone else, children whose lives may be at stake. As for those of you who are now too old to have children, I would ask you to count as gain the greater part of your life, in which you have been happy, and remember that what remains is not long, and let your hearts be lifted up at the thought of the fair fame of the dead. One's sense of honour is the only thing that does not grow old, and the last pleasure, when one is worn out with age, is not, as the poet said, making money, but having the respect of one's fellow men.

"As for those of you here who are sons or brothers of the dead, I can see a hard struggle in front of you. Everyone always speaks well of the dead, and, even if you rise to the greatest heights of heroism, it will be a hard thing for you to get the reputation of having come near, let alone equalled, their standard. When one is alive, one is always liable to the jealousy of one's competitors, but when one is out of the way, the honour one receives is sincere and unchallenged.

"Perhaps I should say a word or two on the duties of women to those among you who are now widowed. I can say all I have to say in a short word of advice. Your great glory is not to be inferior to what God has made you, and the greatest glory of a woman is to be least talked about by men, whether they are praising you or criticizing you. I have now, as the law demanded, said what I had to say. For the time being our offerings to the dead have been made, and for the future their children will be supported at the public expense by the city, until they come of age. This is the crown and prize which she offers, both to the dead and to their children, for the ordeals which they have faced. Where the rewards of valour are the greatest, there you will find also the best and bravest spirits among the people. And now, when you have mourned for your dear ones, you must depart."

12   *John Stuart Mill: A Liberal Praises Athenian Democracy*

Despite the beauty and force of Pericles' tribute to popular rule, one should never forget that Thucydides himself, like many of his compatriots, held a lifelong and profound distrust for democracy unless it was actually, as under Pericles, "the rule of one man." The best form of government, as far as the historian was concerned, was like the one created for a brief time after the oligarchic revolution of 411, when the franchise was limited to holders of a certain amount of property.

In fact, to the English political philosopher Thomas Hobbes (1588– 1679), the principal value of Thucydides' history was to expose and discredit the democratic form of government. As a young man, Hobbes had translated Thucydides, and he describes his reaction to the historian in his autobiography as follows:[1]

"Among the Greek Historians Thucydides delighted me beyond all others, and gradually during my leisure hours I made a translation which was widely appreciated and which I published about 1628 in order that the folly of the Athenian democrats and their fellow citizens be made apparent."

And again:

"He [sc. Thucydides] showed me how stupid Democracy is, and how much wiser is one man than an assemblage. I translated this writer that he might advise Englishmen to avoid the counsel of orators."

Whereas Thomas Hobbes sought to justify the supremacy of state and society over the individual, the very opposite was argued two centuries later by a man whose intellectual gifts and whose lucid and

---

[1] Translated from the Latin by the editor.

compelling understanding of the real meaning of individual liberty made him the true founder of modern liberalism.

John Stuart Mill (1806–1873) must be considered a genius by any standard; he could read classical Greek at the age of six and spent childhood and adolescence in a relentless pursuit of knowledge. Few men in the history of the world have been as superbly educated as Mill, and even fewer have used their education to such advantage. By the time he had reached young manhood, he had already formulated the concept of liberalism which he defended so strenuously for the rest of his life: the idea that the individual was superior to any state, and was answerable to the state only insofar as his unfettered freedom imposed on others.

Mill and his followers were a tiny minority in an age that supported the idea of parliamentary government but supposed it to be the exclusive preserve of a chosen elite. When another great nineteenth century liberal, George Grote (1794–1871), wrote his massive twelve volume History of Greece, *which appeared between 1846 and 1856, he continually reminded his readers that admiration of the Athenian democracy was not currently in vogue, nor had it been for many centuries. In a review of his friend's work, Mill was quick to second Grote's appreciation of Athenian democracy's true achievements, and he noted with some asperity that only a real democracy allows itself the luxury of permitting its most vicious enemies—in this case, the Athenian oligarchs—not only to live in freedom, but to preach the rule of the Few and to compete for the highest offices in the state. Today, we take for granted this freedom of speech for even the most dangerous crackpots; we must view the fact that Mill considered such free expression a novelty in his day as an indication of the progress liberalism has made.*

The intellectual and moral pre-eminence which made Athens the centre of good to Greece, and of the good to after-generations of which Greece has been the medium, was wholly the

SOURCE. From the *Edinburgh Review*, October, 1853. Reprinted in *Dissertations and Discussions* iii (Boston, 1865), pp. 217–224.

fruit of Athenian institutions. It was the consequence, first of democracy, and secondly of the wise and well-considered organization by which the Athenian democracy was distinguished among the democratic constitutions of antiquity. The term "democracy" may perhaps be deemed inapplicable to any of the Grecian governments, on account of the existence of slavery; and it is inapplicable to them in the purest and most honourable sense of the term. But in another sense, not altogether inappropriate, those governments, the first to which the word "democracy" was applied, must be considered entitled to the name: in the same manner as it is given to the Northern States of America, although women are there excluded from the rights of citizenship; an exclusion which, equally with that of slaves, militates against the democratic principle. The Athenian Constitution was so far a democracy, that it was government by a multitude, composed in majority of poor persons—small landed proprietors and artisans. It had the additional democratic characteristic, far more practically important than even the political franchise—it was a government of boundless publicity and freedom of speech. It had the liberty of the bema, of the dicastery, the portico, the palæstra, and the stage; altogether a full equivalent for the liberty of the press. Further, it was the *only* government of antiquity which possessed this inestimable advantage in the same degree, or retained it as long. Enemies and friends alike testify that the outspokenness of Athens was paralleled in no other place in the known world. Every office and honor was open to every citizen, not, as in the aristocratic Roman republic (or even the British monarchy), almost nominally, but really; while the daily working of Athenian institutions (by means of which every citizen was accustomed to hear every sort of question, public and private, discussed by the ablest men of the time, with the earnestness of purpose, and fulness of preparation, belonging to actual business, deliberative or judicial) formed a course of political education, the equivalent of which modern nations have not known how to give even to those whom they educate for statesmen. To their multitudinous judicial tribunals the Athenians were also indebted for that habitual love of fair play, and of hearing both sides of a case, which was more or less a quality of the Greeks generally, but had so firm a hold on the Athenians, that it did not desert them under the most passionate excitement. The potency of Grecian democracy in making every individual in the multitude identify his feelings and interests with those of the State, and regard its freedom and greatness as the first and principal of his own personal concerns, cannot be better described than in the words of Mr. Grote. After quoting a remarkable passage from Herodotus, descriptive of the unexpected outburst of patriotic energy at Athens after the expulsion of the Pisistratidæ, and the establishment of the Cleisthenean Constitution,[1] Mr. Grote proceeds as follows:

"Democracy in Grecian antiquity possessed the privilege, not only of kindling an earnest and unanimous attachment to the constitution in the bosoms of the citizens, but also of creating an energy of public and private action such as could never be obtained under an oligarchy, where the utmost that could be hoped for was a passive acquiescence and obedience. Mr. Burke has remarked, that the mass of the people are generally very indifferent about theories of government: but such indifference (although improvements in the practical working of all governments tend to foster it) is hardly to be expected among any people who exhibit decided mental activity and spirit on other matters; and the reverse was unquestionably true, in the year 500 B.C., among the communities of ancient Greece. Theories of government were there any thing but a dead letter: they were connected with emotions of the strongest as well as of the most opposite character. The theory of a permanent ruling One, for example, was universally odious: that of a ruling Few, though acquiesced in, was never positively attractive, unless either where it was associated with the maintenance of peculiar education and habits, as at Sparta, or where it presented itself as the only antithesis to democracy; the latter having, by peculiar circumstances, become an object of

---

[1] "It is clear not from one thing but from many that equality is an excellent matter; for the Athenians while under one master were in no way better in war than their neighbors, but having cast off tyranny they became far superior. In this case it is clear that under subjection they were willing cowards because they were working for a master, but gaining freedom, each was eager to work in his own interest." (V, 78) Mill originally supplied this passage in Greek; it is translated here by the editor.

terror. But the theory of democracy was pre-eminently seductive; creating in the mass of the citizens an intense positive attachment, and disposing them to voluntary action and suffering on its behalf, such as no coercion on the part of other governments could entail. Herodotus, in his comparison of the three sorts of government,[2] puts in the front rank of the advantages of democracy "its most splendid name and promise"—its power of enlisting the hearts of the citizens in support of their constitution, and of providing for all a common bond of union and fraternity. This is what even democracy did not always do; but it was what no other government in Greece *could* do—a reason alone sufficient to stamp it as the best government, and presenting the greatest chance of beneficent results. . . . Among the Athenian citizens, certainly, it produced a strength and unanimity of positive political sentiment such as has rarely been seen in the history of mankind; which excites our surprise and admiration the more, when we compare it with the apathy which had preceded, and which is even implied as the natural state of the public mind in Solon's famous proclamation against neutrality in a sedition. Because democracy happens to be unpalatable to most modern readers, they have been accustomed to look upon the sentiment here described only in its least honorable manifestations—in the caricatures of Aristophanes, or in the empty commonplaces of rhetorical declaimers. But it is not in this way that the force, the earnestness, or the binding value, of democratical sentiment at Athens is to be measured. We must listen to it as it comes from the lips of Pericles, while he is strenuously enforcing upon the people those active duties for which it both implanted the stimulus and supplied the courage; or from the oligarchial Nikias in the harbor of Syracuse, when he is endeavoring to revive the courage of his despairing troops for one last death-struggle, and when he appeals to their democratical patriotism as to the only flame yet alive and burning even in that moment of agony. From the time of Kleisthenes downward, the creation of this new mighty impulse makes an entire revolution in the Athenian character; and, if the change still stood out in so prom-

[2] See pp. 6–10, above.

inent a manner before the eyes of Herodotus, much more must it have been felt by the contemporaries among whom it occurred."

The influences here spoken of were those of democracy generally. For the peculiar and excellent organization of her own democracy. Athens was indebted to a succession of eminent men. The earliest was her great legislator, Solon; himself the first capital prize which Athens drew in the dispensations of the Destinies; a man whose personal virtue ennobled the city by which he was chosen to legislate, and the merit of whose institutions was a principal source of the deep-rooted respect for the laws which distinguished Athens beyond any other of the ancient democracies. The salutary forms of business established by Solon, and calculated to secure as much caution and deliberation as were compatible with ultimate decision by a sovereign Ecclesia, lived through the successive changes by which the constitution was rendered more and more democratic. And though it is commonly supposed that popular passion in a democracy is peculiarly liable to trample on forms when they stand between it and its object—which is indeed, without question, one of the dangers of a democracy—there is no point in the character of the Athenians more remarkable than their respect and attachment to the forms of their constitution. In the height of their anger against Pericles for not leading them out to defend their lands and houses from the ravages of the Peloponnesians—because he, standing on his privilege as a magistrate, abstained from calling an assembly, no assembly met. There is indeed but one marked instance known to us, in Athenian history, of that violation of forms which was the daily practice of most of the oligarchical governments. That one was a case of great and just provocation—the *cause célèbre* of the six generals who neglected to save their drowning countrymen after the seafight of Arginusæ; and there was, as Mr. Grote has shown, no injustice in the fact of their condemnation by the people, though there was a blamable violation of the salutary rules of criminal procedure established for the protection of the innocent. It was in this case that the philosopher Socrates, accidentally that month a senator of the presiding tribe, as firm against the tyranny of the

majority as afterwards against the wrath of a tyrant, singly re-
fused to join in putting the question to the assembly contrary to
the laws; adding one to the proofs that the man of greatest intellect
at that time in Athens was also its most virtuous citizen.

After Solon (omitting the intervening usurpation of Pisistratus),
the first great constitutional change was the reformation of Cleisthenes; an eminent man, to whose character and historical importance no one before Mr. Grote had done justice. The next was that
in which the immediate mover was Aristides, at the reestablish-
ment of the city after the Persian War, when the poorest class
of citizens was first admitted to share in public employments. The
final measures which completed the democratic constitution were
those of Pericles and Ephialtes; more particularly the latter—a
statesman of whom, from the unfortunate absence of any contemporary history of the period between the Persian and Peloponnesian wars except the brief introductory sketch of Thucydides, we
have to lament that too little is known, but of whom the recorded
anecdotes indicate a man worthy to have been the friend of
Pericles. Ephialtes perished by assassination; a victim to the ran-
corous hatred of the oligarchical party. Assassination afterwards
disappears from Athenian public life, until re-introduced on a
regular system by the same party, to effect the revolution of the
Four Hundred. The Athenian Many, of whose democratic irri-
tability and suspicion we hear so much, are rather to be accused
of too easy and good-natured a confidence, when we reflect that
they had living in the midst of them the very men, who, on the
first show of an opportunity, were ready to compass the sub-
version of the democracy. . . . These men ought always to be
present to the mind, not merely as a dark background to the
picture of the Athenian Republic, but as an active power in it.
They were no obscure private individuals, but men of rank and
fortune; not only prominent as politicians and public speakers,
but continually trusted with all the great offices of State. Truly
Athens was in more danger from these men than from the demagogues: they were indeed themselves the worst of the demagogues;
described by Phrynichus, their confederate, as for their own
purposes, the leaders and instigators of the Demos to its most
blamable actions.

13   Eduard Meyer: A German Scholar Blasts Mob Rule

The enthusiasm of Mill and Grote for Athenian democracy was not to be shared by a large audience for more than a century. Far more common were sentiments like the following, by Eduard Meyer (1855–1930), the most respected ancient historian of his day, and one of the last men to attempt a treatment of all antiquity from the Flood to the fall of Rome.

[By the end of the fifth century] the ideal of the [Athenian] state was losing its importance. The defects of the democracy were too obvious; those in particular who insist that the state be the embodiment of an ethical concept must recognize that the democracy made such a concept impossible to implement. In spite of all the beautiful theories of liberty and equality, the democracy was in reality nothing more than a dictatorship of the masses over property owners, and an undisguised exploitation of the state in the interests of the lower classes. The belief that free discussion and the right of anyone to state his opinion must lead to revelation of the truth, and that the sovereign People could intuitively discover what was just, is denied by the actual results; how, in fact, could such a situation be possible under a constitution which entrusted all decisions to an ignorant plurality and suppressed the intelligent and well-to-do? A superior intellect like Pericles might rule the mob for a time and keep it on a sensible course, but the moment this same mob was left to its own designs it demonstrated once again its incompetence and base self-indulgence.

SOURCE. From *Geschichte des Altertums*, Volume IV.1, pp. 786–788. Originally published in 1900. Reprinted by Benno Schwabe & Co., Basel, 1954. Translated by the editor. Reprinted by permission of Benno Schwabe & Co.

The people's tribunals[1] were the palladium of the democracy; but the tragedy is not only the fact that the common man regarded it more his privilege than his duty to sit in judgment and make upright and wealthy men feel his power; that the pay, meager as it was, attracted him as being a welcome supplement to his income —even worse that in these trials unjust verdicts and judicial murders continued to pile up, partly because of ignorance, partly because the jurors were relentlessly guided by their own narrow interests. Already by the time of the Archidamian War [431-21], as Aristophanes attests . . . it was not infrequently the case that the jurors were warned: if they did not condemn a rich defendant, there would be no money for their pay.

The two-edged power of oratory in its full frightfulness is exposed above all in these debates before popular tribunals as well as before popular assemblies. It was indispensable for the public interest that each citizen have the right to intercede to protect the interests of the state from abuse and to bring corrupt officials to trial, for no governmental apparatus existed which could intervene in such cases (nor was such an office thinkable, considering the lines along which the state was modelled). But this led to the emergence of a band of professional informers, or "sycophants" . . . These creatures became the scourge of all respectable men, whom they threatened with indictment on the slightest pretext unless they were bought off with money. Even the Democracy was aware of their destructive potential; the assembly reserved to itself the right to refer annually three of the most extreme accusers to the courts for judgment, by means of a motion of censure. But this grotesque procedure only goes to show the inevitability of the evil, and illustrates drastically at the same time how far justice had given way to expediency.

No one can blame the Athenian masses for clinging to a constitution which served them so very well; but a large segment of the educated and upper classes as well remained true to the concept of the democracy (which was inextricably bound to the concept of the Athenian state) no matter how keenly they felt

---

[1] The citizen juries of 501 or more, appointed by lot and paid a small wage for their time and effort. *Ed.*

the abuses. They only asked for restraint, elimination of corrupt practices and a sort of compromise arrangement by which some legitimate influence would continue to be entrusted to the upper classes and property owners. This frame of mind often finds expression in Euripides, and all conservative statesmen after Pericles acknowledged the situation at least tacitly. But there was emerging at the same time a radical-oligarchic party which strove in every way available for the overthrow of the existing order, and no longer hesitated to betray the country when no other method offered itself to save the homeland from tyranny of the rabble and to restore the ideal conditions of the old days.

14 *A. H. M. Jones: Ancient Critics and a Modern Defense*

The greatest minds of antiquity had been almost unanimous in their denunciation of democracy, and it has been all too easy for more recent commentators to take their criticism at face value. But the experience of the twentieth century with totalitarian government has helped to temper such outright rejection.

The following selection is a masterly analysis of all the evidence by a historian and authority on ancient society and institutions from Cambridge University. Professor A. H. M. Jones has written widely on ancient cities, economics, Athenian and Roman law and government.

It is curious that in the abundant literature produced in the greatest democracy of Greece there survives no statement of

SOURCE. A. H. M. Jones, "The Athenian Democracy and its Critics," *Cambridge Historical Journal* 9 (1953), pp. 1–26. Reprinted in *Athenian Democracy*, Oxford: Blackwell, 1957, pp. 41–72. Copyright 1953. Reprinted by permission of Basil Blackwell & Mott, Ltd.

democratic political theory. All the Athenian political philosophers and publicists whose works we possess were in various degrees oligarchic in sympathy. The author of the pamphlet on the "Constitution of the Athenians" preserved among Xenophon's works is bitterly hostile to democracy. Socrates, so far as we can trace his views from the works of Xenophon and Plato, was at least highly critical of democracy. Plato's views on the subject are too well known to need stating. Isocrates in his earlier years wrote panegyrics of Athens, but in his old age, when he wrote his more philosophical works, became increasingly embittered against the political régime of his native city. Aristotle is the most judicial in his attitude, and states the pros and cons, but his ideal was a widely based oligarchy. With the historians of Athens, the same bias is evident. Only Herodotus is a democrat, but his views have not carried much weight, partly because of his reputation for naïveté, and partly because his explicit evidence refers to a period before the full democracy had evolved. Thucydides is hostile: in one of the very few passages in which he reveals his personal views he expresses approval of a régime which disfranchised about two-thirds of the citizens, those who manned the fleet on which the survival of Athens depended. Xenophon was an ardent admirer of the Spartan régime. Aristotle, in the historical part of his monograph on the Constitution of Athens, followed—rather uncritically—a source with a marked oligarchic bias. Only the fourth-century orators were democrats; and their speeches, being concerned with practical political issues—mostly of foreign policy —or with private litigation, have little to say on the basic principles of democracy, which they take for granted.

The surviving literature is certainly not representative of Athenian public opinion. The majority of Athenians were proud of their constitution and deeply attached to it. The few counter-revolutions—in 411, 404, 322 and 317—were carried out by small extremist cliques, in 411 after a carefully planned campaign of deception and terror, in the other three cases with the aid of a foreign conqueror, and all were short-lived, being rapidly overwhelmed by the mass of the citizens. Nor was it only the poor majority, who most obviously benefited from the system, that were its supporters. Most of the great statesmen and generals of

Athens came from wealthy families, and a substantial number from the nobility of birth; the leaders of the popular rising which unseated the oligarchic governments of 411 and 403 were men of substance.

Since, however, the majority were mute—in the literature which has survived—it is not an easy task to discern what they considered the merits of democracy to be, or, indeed, on what principles they thought that a good constitution should be based. Democratic political theory can only be tentatively reconstructed from scattered allusions. For the basic ideals of democracy the best source is the series of panegyrics on Athens. The most famous of these, Pericles' Funeral Speech, as recorded by Thucydides, is also the most instructive; its peculiarities of diction and its general tone, which is in conflict with Thucydides' own outlook, suggest that it is a fairly faithful reproduction of what Pericles really said. There is an early fourth-century Funeral Speech attributed to Lysias, which contains some useful material. Little for our purposes can be drawn from Isocrates' *Panegyricus* and *Panathenaicus*. A curious document of this class is the skit on a Funeral Speech contained in Plato's *Menexenus*, which seems close enough to type to be used—with reservations—as a statement of democratic principles. To these documents, which too often only repeat banal generalities, may be added *obiter dicta* in the political and forensic speeches of the orators, when they appeal to some general principle. Among these may be included some political speeches in Thucydides, which, though placed in a Sicilian setting, doubtless are modelled on Athenian prototypes. Another important source is the actual constitution of Athens, from whose rules general principles can sometimes be deduced. But our most valuable evidence comes from the criticisms of adversaries, which are so much more fully reported than anything from the democratic side. This evidence, though copious, is tricky to evaluate and must be used with caution. We must distinguish criticism on points of principle, where a democrat would have accepted his opponent's statement of the democratic point of view as correct, and would have argued that the principle or institution criticised was in fact a good one; and criticism on points of practice, which a democrat would have endeavoured to rebut, arguing that the accusations were untrue, or alternatively that the abuses alleged were regrettable but accidental and remediable defects of democracy.

It is the object of this paper to reconstruct from these sources democratic political theory and then to determine how far in practice the Athenian people lived up to its principles. The procedure will be to take up the various lines of criticism advanced by oligarchic critics, and to work out on what lines democrats would have answered them, using for this purpose the scattered evidence outlined above. The criticisms of the philosophical writers will be analysed first, and then those of the historians—or rather of Thucydides, who alone demands discussion. This distinction in the source of the criticism corresponds with a division in subject-matter, for the philosophers confine their attacks almost entirely to the internal working of democracy, while Thucydides is primarily interested in Athenian foreign and imperial policy.

The first and most basic charge brought by the philosophers against democracy is best expressed by Aristotle in his characteristic terse direct style: "in such democracies each person lives as he likes: or in the words of Euripides 'according to his fancy.' This is a bad thing." This is no isolated text. Aristotle returns to the point elsewhere. Isocrates in the *Areopagiticus* declares that in the good old days it was not the case that the citizens "had many supervisors in their education but as soon as they reached man's estate were allowed to do what they liked," and urges that the Areopagus should recover its alleged pristine power of controlling the private lives of all the citizens. Plato in the *Republic* complains that under a democracy "the city is full of liberty and free speech and everyone in it is allowed to do what he likes . . . each man in it could plan his own life as he pleases." He then enlarges on the deplorable results of this, that the citizens are various, instead of conforming to one type, and that foreigners and even women and slaves are as free as the citizens.

An Athenian democrat would no doubt have demurred at the last charge, though admitting with some pride that foreigners and slaves were exceptionally well treated at Athens, but he certainly gloried in the accusation of liberty. Freedom of action and of speech were the proudest slogans of Athens, and not only political but personal freedom; as Pericles says in the Funeral Speech, "we live as free citizens both in our public life and in our attitude to one another in the affairs of daily life; we are not angry with our neighbour if he behaves as he pleases, we do not cast sour looks at him, which, if they can do no harm, cause pain." Freedom of speech was particularly prized. As Demosthenes says, "in Sparta you are not allowed to praise the laws of Athens or of this state or that, far from it, you have to praise what agrees with their constitution," whereas in Athens criticism of the democracy was freely permitted. One only has to read the works of Isocrates, Plato and Aristotle to see that this is true. The condemnation of Socrates is an apparent exception to the rule, but as Xenophon's account of the matter shows, the real gravamen of the charge against Socrates was that, of his pupils, Alcibiades had done more than any other one man to ruin Athens in the recent war, and Critias had been the ruthless ringleader of the Thirty, who had massacred thousands of Athenians a few years before.

The second main charge against democracy is most neatly stated by Plato: that "it distributes a kind of equality to the equal and the unequal alike." The same point is made by Isocrates, who distinguishes "two equalities; one allots the same to every one and the other what is appropriate to each," and alleges that in the good old days the Athenians "rejected as unjust the equality which considers the good and the bad worthy of the same rights, and chose that which honours each according to his worth." Aristotle argues similarly, though he is justifiably sceptical about the criterion according to which rights are to be scaled; in democracy freedom is the criterion, that is, all free men are equal, and this is in Aristotle's view unjust, but so in his opinion are the only practical alternative criteria, wealth or birth.

Democrats in general approved of the egalitarian principle. Demosthenes in one passage argues that what makes all citizens public spirited and generous is "that in a democracy each man considers that he himself has a share in equality and justice," and in another praises a law forbidding legislation directed against individuals as being good democratic doctrine, "for as everyone has an equal share in the rest of the constitution, so everyone is entitled to an equal share in the laws." The Athenians were not, however, either in theory or in practice, absolute egalitarians, but drew a distinction between different political functions. On one point they admitted no compromise—equality before the law; as Pericles says, "in their private disputes all share equality according to the laws." This to us elementary principle needed emphasis, for Plato's friends in the Thirty, when they drew up a new constitution, ordained that only the 3,000 full citizens were entitled to a legal trial and that all others might be summarily executed by order of the government. It was secured in the Athenian constitution not only by the right of every citizen to seek redress in the courts, but by the character of the courts, which consisted of large juries drawn by lot from the whole body of the citizens.

The Athenians also attached great importance to the equality of all citizens in formulating and deciding public policy. This was secured by the right of every citizen to speak and vote in the assembly, and by the composition of the council of Five Hundred, which prepared the agenda of the assembly; this body was annually chosen by lot from all the demes of Attica. Here democratic principle came into conflict with the oligarchic view, developed at length by Plato, that government was an art, demanding the highest skill, and should therefore be entrusted to a select few. On this question Aristotle, whose ideal was a broadly based oligarchy, whose members would not all be experts, took issue with Plato, and the arguments which he uses are applicable to a fully democratic régime, and probably drawn from democratic theory. In the first place he argues that, though each individual in a large assembly may be of poor quality, the sum of their virtue and wisdom taken together may exceed the virtue and wisdom of a select few, just as dinners provided by joint contributions may be better than those provided by one rich host. His second argument is rather most cogent. Politics, he suggests, is one of those arts in which the best judge is not the artist himself but the user of the product. The householder is a better judge of a house than the architect, the steersman of a rudder rather than the carpenter, the eater of a meal rather than the cook. A third justification for democratic practice is put into the mouth of Protagoras by Plato in a passage which so well illustrates the tone of the Athenian assembly that it is worth quoting in full. Socrates is expressing his doubts as to whether political wisdom is teachable.

"I, like the other Greeks (he says), think that the Athenians are wise. Well, I see that when we gather for the assembly, when the city has to do something about buildings, they call for the builders as advisers and when it is about ship construction, the shipwrights, and so on with everything else that can be taught and learned. And if anyone else tries to advise them, whom they do not think an expert, even if he be quite a gentleman, rich and aristocratic, they none the less refuse to listen, but jeers and boo, until either the speaker himself is shouted down and gives up, or the sergeants at arms, on the order of the presidents, drag him off or remove him. That is how they behave on technical questions. But when the debate is on the general government of the city, anyone gets up and advises them, whether he be a carpenter or a smith or a leather worker, a merchant or a sea-captain, rich or poor, noble or humble, and no one blames them like the others for trying to give advice, when they have not learned from any source and have no teacher."

Protagoras' reply is in mythological form. Zeus when he created men gave various talents to each, but to all he gave a sense of decency and fair play, since without them any society would be impossible.

"So, Socrates, (he concludes) that is why the Athenians and the others, when the debate is about architecture or any other technical question, think that few should take part in the discussion, and if anyone outside the few joins in, do not tolerate it, as you say—rightly in my opinion. But when they come to discuss political questions, which must be determined by justice and moderation, they properly listen to everyone, thinking that everyone shares in these qualities—or cities wouldn't exist."

The Athenians went yet further in their egalitarian principles in that they entrusted the routine administration of the city to boards of magistrates chosen by lot. This aroused the irony of Socrates, who declared that "it was silly that the rulers of the city should be appointed by lot, when no one would be willing to employ a pilot or a carpenter or a flautist chosen by lot." It is a proof of the poverty of our information on democratic theory that no reasoned defence of this cardinal institution, the lot, has survived. The nearest thing to it is a comic passage in a private speech of Demosthenes where Mantitheus, pleading against the assumption of his name by his half-brother, raises the hypothetical case that both might put in their names for the ballot for an office or the council, and that the name Mantitheus might be drawn. There would have to be a lawsuit "and we shall be deprived of our common equality, that the man who wins the ballot holds office: we shall abuse one another and the cleverer speaker will hold the office." It is implied that the lot was employed to give every citizen an equal chance, without regard to wealth, birth or even popularity or eloquence. This may seem to be carrying principle to extremes, but Socrates' comment is not altogether fair. It was not "the rulers of the city" who were chosen by lot, but officials charged with limited routine duties, for which little more than "a sense of decency and fair play" was required. Furthermore, it must be remembered that a magistrate had to pass a preliminary examination, which was, it is true, usually formal, but gave his enemies an opportunity for raking up his past; was liable to be deposed by a vote of the assembly taken ten times a year; and after his year was subject to a scrutiny in which his accounts were audited and any citizen could charge him with inefficiency or abuse of authority. It is unlikely that many rogues or nincompoops would expose themselves to these risks.

Athenian democrats did not believe that all should share alike in the important offices, whose holders to some extent controlled policy. Pericles, after affirming the equality before the law of all citizens, goes on: "but in public esteem, when a man is distinguished in any way, he is more highly honoured in public life, not as a matter of privilege but in recognition of merit; on the other hand any one who can benefit the city is not debarred by poverty or by the obscurity of his position." This point is even more strongly put in the mock panegyric in the *Menexenus*.

"For in the main the same constitution existed then as now, an aristocracy, under which we now live and have always lived since then. A man may call it democracy, and another what he will. But in truth it is an aristocracy with the approval of the majority. We have always had kings: sometimes they were hereditary, sometimes elective. In most things the majority is in control of the city, and bestows office and power on those whom it thinks to be the best. No one is rejected for weakness or poverty or humble birth, nor honoured for their opposites, as in other cities. There is one criterion: the man who is thought to be wise and good holds power and rule."

These principles were embodied in the Athenian constitution, whereby all the important magistrates—the ten generals, who not only commanded the army and the fleet but exercised a general control over defence and foreign policy, the other military commanders, and in the fourth century the principal financial magistrates—were elected by the people; a procedure which could be regarded as aristocratic. In fact, the Athenian people were rather snobbish in their choice of leaders. The "Old Oligarch" sneeringly remarks, "they do not think that they ought to share by lot in the offices of general or commander of the horse, for the people knows that it gains more by not holding these offices itself but allowing the leading citizens to hold them." Xenophon records the complaints of Nicomachides, an experienced soldier, that he has been beaten in the election for the generalship by a rich man who knows nothing about military affairs. Demosthenes, a strong democrat, rakes up Aeschines' humble origins in a fashion which we should hardly consider in good taste, but apparently did not offend an Athenian jury. "We have judged you, a painter of alabaster boxes and drums, and these junior clerks and nobodies (and there is no harm in such occupations, but on the other hand they are not deserving of a generalship) worthy of ambassadorships, generalships and the highest honours."

Besides the lot the other instrument whereby the Athentians secured the effective political equality of the citizens was pay. The 6000 jurors, the council of 500 and the 350 odd magistrates were all paid for their services at various rates; it may be noted that elective magistrates—the military commanders and ambassadors—were paid, and at higher rates than the ordinary magistrates chosen by lot, so that the real claim that poverty was no barrier to political power was justified. During the fourth century citizens who attended the assembly—or at least a quorum who arrived first—were also paid. The philosophers objected to this practice. Aristotle criticises it precisely because it fulfilled its purpose of enabling the poor to exercise their political rights. It may, however, be doubted if by his day it was fully effective. The assembly and the juries seem, from the tone in which the orators address them, to have consisted predominantly of middle-class citizens rather than of the poor, and there is evidence that the council also was mainly filled by the well-to-do. The real value of the State pay had, owing to the progressive rise of prices, sunk considerably by the latter part of the fourth century, and the poor probably preferred more profitable employment. Plato also objects to State pay: "I am told," he says, "that Pericles made the Athenians idle and lazy and garrulous and avaricious by first putting them on State pay." This is an oft-repeated accusation but has very little substance. In a population which never sank below 20,000 adult males and probably reached twice that figure at its peak, the council and the magistracies did not provide employment except on rare occasions; a man might not hold any magistracy more than once, or sit on the council more than twice in his life. Assemblies were held only on forty days in the year. It was only as a juror that a citizen could obtain more or less continuous employment, and here the rate of remuneration was so low—half a labourer's wage in the fifth century and a third in the late fourth, in fact little more than bare subsistence—that in the fifth century, if the picture drawn in Aristophane's *Wasps* is true, it attracted only the elderly, past hard work, and in the early fourth century, when economic conditions were worse, according to Isocrates, the unemployed.

The third main criticism of democracy comes from Aristotle, that in its extreme (that is, Athenian) form "the mass of the people (or the 'majority') is sovereign instead of the law; this happens when decrees are valid instead of the law." It is not entirely clear what Aristotle means by this. He appears here and elsewhere to conceive of the law as an immutable code, laid down by an impartial legislator, against which the will of the citizens, assumed

always to be self-interested, should not in an ideal State be allowed to prevail. He may therefore be objecting to any legislation by decision of the majority—or, for that matter, by any
constitutional procedure. But this meaning seems to slide into
another, that in an extreme democracy the majority in the assembly habitually overrides the existing laws, however established, by
arbitrary executive action in particular cases, acting, as he puts it,
like the traditional Greek tyrant.

The doctrine of the immobility of law was naturally favoured
by oligarchs, who were generally conservative, or, when they
wanted to alter the law, professed to be restoring an "ancestral
constitution." Democrats, who more often wished to change
things, might have been expected to work out a more progressive
theory. Some thinkers in the fifth century did indeed propound
the doctrine that the law was the will of the sovereign. Socrates,
according to Xenophon, defined law as "what the citizens have by
agreement enacted on what must be done and what avoided," and
was quite prepared to admit that what the citizens enacted they
could revoke, just as having declared war they could make peace.
Xenophon also reports a no doubt imaginary conversation between
Pericles and Alcibiades, in which the former defined law as "what
the mass of the people (or 'the majority'), having come together
and approved it, decrees, declaring what must and what must not
be done." Led on by Alcibiades he extends this definition to oligarchies and tyrannies, declaring that what the sovereign body or
person decrees is law. Asked by Alcibiades what then is violence
and lawlessness, Pericles replies "when the stronger does not persuade the weaker but compels him by force to do what he wants."
This enables Alcibiades after suitable leading questions about tyrants and oligarchies, to ask: "Would what the whole mass of the
people, overpowering the holders of property, enacts without
persuading them, be violence rather than law?" Pericles at this
point tells Alcibiades to go away and play, leaving the ambiguity
in his theory of law unresolved. In the fourth century Demosthenes enunciates a similar view in one passage, asserting that "the
laws lay down about the future (he is denouncing retrospective
legislation as undemocratic) what must be done, being enacted
by persuasion as they will benefit their users." Some democrats

then conceived of law as the considered will of the majority, adding the rider that the majority should persuade the minority and consider the interests of all.

In general, however, democrats tended like Aristotle to regard the laws as a code laid down once for all by a wise legislator, in their case Solon, which, immutable in principle, might occasionally require to be clarified or supplemented. These were the terms of reference given to the legislative commission set up after the restoration of the democracy in 403, and the standing rules governing legislation show the same spirit. At no time was it legal to alter the law by a simple decree of the assembly. The mover of such a decree was liable to the famous "indictment for illegal proceedings," which, if upheld by the courts, quashed the decree, and also, if brought within a year, exposed the mover to heavy penalties. In the fifth century additions to the law were prepared by special legislative commissions, and then submitted to the council and assembly, but there seems to have been no constitutional means of altering the existing law. After 403 an elaborate procedure was introduced for revising the law, which took the matter out of the hands of the assembly. Every year the assembly passed the laws under review, and voted on them, section by section, whether they should stand or be revised. If a revision of any section was voted, any citizen was entitled to propound alternative laws, which were given due publicity, and a court of 501 or 1,001 legislators was empanelled. The issue between the old and the proposed laws was then argued judicially (counsel for the old laws being appointed by the assembly), and the legislators, acting as a jury under oath, gave their verdict.

Such was the Athenian theory on legislation. How far it was observed in practice is disputable. Both Demosthenes and Aeschines, when bringing indictments for illegal proceedings, inveigh against the unscrupulous politicians (their opponents) who flout the law, and Demosthenes alleges that as a result "there are so many contradictory laws that you have for a long while past been electing commissions to resolve the conflict, and none the less the problem can have no end. Laws are no different from decrees, and the laws, according to which decrees ought to be indicted, are more recent than the decrees themselves." These

strictures may be taken with a grain of salt. Politicians no doubt
often tried to by-pass the rather cumbrous procedure for legislation—Demosthenes did so himself through Apollodorus over the
allocation of the theoric fund. But the indictment for illegal proceedings was a favourite political weapon, often invoked, as by
Aeschines against Demosthenes on the famous issue of the Crown,
on very technical grounds. And Aristophon's boast that he had
been indicted (unsuccessfully) seventy-five times, if it proves
that some politicians often sailed near the wind, also proves that
there were many jealous watchdogs of the constitution; Demosthenes' attempt to evade the law was, incidentally, foiled and
Apollodorus suffered.

On the other aspect of the rule of law Athenian democrats held
exactly the opposite view to Aristotle's. "Tyrannies and oligarchies," according to Aeschines, "are governed by the ways of their
governments, democratic cities by the established laws." "No one,
I think, would assert," says Demosthenes, "that there is any more
important cause for the blessings which the city enjoys and for
its being democratic and free, than the laws." In another passage
Demosthenes contrasts law and oligarchy, declaring that in the
latter any member of the government can revoke existing rules
and make arbitrary enactments about the future, whereas the
laws lay down what must be done for the future and are passed
by persuasion in the interests of all. To Lycurgus of "the three
most important factors which maintain and preserve democracy,"
the first is the law. Hypereides declares it all-important "that in
a democracy the laws shall be sovereign."

Both sides were naturally thinking of the worst specimens of
the opposite party. Athenian democrats inevitably called to mind
the arbitrary excesses of their own Four Hundred and Thirty
when they spoke of oligarchies, and oligarchs could no doubt cite
democracies whose acts were as brutal and illegal. On the whole
the Athenian democracy seems to have lived up to its principles.
Xenophon has given us a vivid picture of one occasion when the
assembly in a hysterical mood rode roughshod over its own rules
of procedure and condemned the generals in command at Argi-
nusae to death by one summary vote. But the emphasis given to
this incident suggests that it was very exceptional. And Xenophon,

no favourable witness to the democracy, also testifies that after the restoration of the democracy in 403 the people religiously observed the amnesty agreed with the supporters of the Thirty. When one reads Xenophon's and Aristotle's record of the doings of the Thirty, one cannot but be amazed at the steadfast forbearance of the Athenian people.

The final and principal charge brought by the philosophers against democracy was that it meant the rule of the poor majority over the rich minority in their own interest. This is the main thesis of the "Old Oligarch," whose treatise on the Athenian constitution takes the form of an ironical appreciation of its efficiency in promoting the interests of "the bad" (the poor) at the expense of "the good" (the rich); he is equally cynical in assuming that 'the good', if they got the chance, would govern in their own interest to the detriment of "the bad." Plato in the *Republic* declares that "democracy results when the poor defeat the others and kill or expel them and share the constitution and the offices equally with the rest." Aristotle is very insistent that democracy is directed to the advantage of the indigent, going so far as to say that if, *per impossibile*, there should be more rich than poor in a city, the rule of the poor minority should be called democracy, and that of the rich majority oligarchy.

This view was naturally not accepted by democrats. Their views are doubtless reflected in the speech put into the mouth of the Syracusan democrat Athenagoras by Thucydides:

"It will be said that democracy is neither wise nor fair, and that the possessors of property are best qualified to rule well. My opinion is first that the people is the name of the whole, and oligarchy of a part, and secondly that the rich are the best guardians of property, the wise the best councillors, and the masses can best hear and judge, and that all these elements alike, jointly and severally, have an equal share in democracy."

It is more difficult to answer the question whether the Athenian democracy did or did not in fact exploit the rich for the benefit of the poor. In the distribution of political power and influence the rich seem to have fared well. In the minor offices and on the council and in the juries the poor no doubt predominated, though

even here it would seem that by the fourth century the well-to-do
were by no means crowded out. To the important military, diplo-
matic and financial offices men of birth and wealth were generally
elected. The orators, who, normally holding no office, guided
policy by their speeches in the assembly were also mostly well-to-
do, and many of them of good family. It was comparatively rarely
that a self-made man like Phrynichus or Aeschines achieved political influence. A rich man or an aristocrat certainly did not find
that his political career was prejudiced by his wealth or birth,
while poor and humbly born politicians had to face a good deal
of abuse from comedians and orators.

Isocrates complains bitterly of the fiscal exploitation of the rich.
In the *de Pace* he rolls out a list of taxes and charges "which cause
so much vexation that property owners lead a harder life than
utter paupers," and in the *Antidosis* he declares: "when I was a
boy it was thought to be such a secure and grand thing to be rich
that practically everyone pretended to possess a larger property
than he actually did, in his desire to acquire this reputation. But
now one has to prepare a defence to prove that one is not rich, as
if it were a great crime." From the meagre figures which we
possess it is difficult to check these allegations. Normal peace-
time expenditure (including the pay of citizens for political services) was defrayed from a variety of indirect taxes, a tax on
resident aliens, royalties from the silver mines, rents of public and
sacred land, court fees and fines and confiscations imposed by the
courts. Certain religious festivals were financed by the system of
liturgies, whereby rich men were nominated to produce plays,
train teams of athletes and the like. In time of war it was often
necessary to raise a property tax, which fell, it would seem, on
about 6,000 persons, or a third to a quarter of the citizen body.
In war time also the richest of the citizens were nominated as
trierarchs, in which capacity they had to maintain a trireme in
seaworthy condition for a year.

The war tax, of which great complaints were made, averaged
over twenty years in the fourth century at a rate equivalent to a
2½¢ to the dollar tax. We need not therefore take the laments
of Isocrates and his like very seriously. The tax seems in fact to
have been too widely spread, and did cause hardship to the poorest

of those liable. It was, as appears from Demosthenes' speeches, very difficult to get the assembly, a substantial proportion of whom were taxpayers, to vote a levy, and hence wars were always inadequately financed. Liturgies are much more difficult to calculate, as it depended greatly on the individual concerned how often he undertook them and how much he spent on each. It was useful political advertisement, almost a form of canvassing, to put up good shows, and rich men were often very willing to acquire popularity by serving frequently and spending lavishly on gorgeous costumes and high salaries to stars. An evidently very rich man for whom Lysias wrote a speech boasts that he undertook eleven liturgies in six years, spending in all nearly 3½ talents—a middle-class fortune. But, as he remarks, he need not have spent on them a quarter of this sum if he had confined himself to the strict requirements of the law; nor need he have performed more than a maximum of four liturgies. At the other extreme another very rich man, Meidias, had, according to Demosthenes, performed only one liturgy at the age of nearly fifty, and Dicaeogenes, another wealthy man, only undertook two minor ones in ten years. The trierarchy was a heavier burden than the ordinary liturgies, costing from 40 to 60 minae (⅔ to 1 talent) a year, and as it might fall on fortunes of 5 talents, the temporary strain on a poor trierarch's resources would be severe. For this reason the burden was usually from the end of the fifth century shared between two holders, and from 357 the 1200 persons liable to trierarchic service were divided into twenty groups, whose members shared the expense: thus, if a fleet of 100 ships were commissioned, twelve men would share the charge for each trierarchy. Here again the incidence of the burden varied greatly. The same man who performed eleven liturgies served seven years as trierarch during the Ionian war, spending 6 talents, and a certain Aristophanes (with his father) served three trierarchies in four or five years in the Corinthian War, spending 80 minae in all. Isocrates, on the other hand, who complains so bitterly of the oppression of the rich, and had made a large fortune by his rhetorical teaching, could at the age of 80 boast of only three trierarchies (including those performed by his son). But it would be unfair to the Athenian upper classes to take the parsimonious orator as typical. As a public-spirited citizen we may instance the father of one of Lysias' clients, who in a career of fifty years (which included the Peloponnesian and Corinthian wars) was trierarch seven times. His son proudly displayed to the jury his father's accounts, which showed that he had altogether disbursed on trierarchies, liturgies and war tax 9 talents 20 minae, an average of over 11 minae per annum. His fortune is not stated, but he certainly was a very rich man, since he entered chariots for the Isthmia and Nemea, and is likely to have possessed substantially more than 15 talents, which Demosthenes implies would qualify a man to be called really rich. If so, his contribution to the state would not have exceeded one-eighth of his income.

The taxation of the rich was very erratic, falling heavily in war years, and was badly distributed; before 357 all persons on the trierarchic register took their turn, though some were much richer than others, and after 357 all members of a group contributed equally. This lack of system enabled some rich men to escape very lightly, and was on occasions oppressive to those with moderate fortunes. On the other hand, many rich men liked to make a splash, undertaking more trierarchies and liturgies than their legal quota, and thereby easing the burden of the others. In general, it it would seem that the average burden borne by the well-to-do in Athens was well within their means, though its erratic incidence might cause them temporary embarrassment.

The critics, however, allege that a more sinister method of soaking the rich than taxation was in vogue at Athens—that of condemning them on trumped-up charges and confiscating their property. There is reason to believe that this abuse of the law courts did sometimes occur, but it is very difficult to say whether it was common.

Some general considerations need to be clarified. Athens, like all ancient States, relied for the enforcement of the law on the services of informers, and was obliged to reward them for convictions. Professional informers seem to have been a pest at Athens; but so they were everywhere—one has only to think of the reputation of *delatores* in imperial Rome. The State did not encourage frivolous accusations, subjecting to severe penalties an informer who failed to win a fifth of the jury's votes, or who abandoned a

prosecution which he had instituted. Nor does it appear that informers were popular with juries. Defendants try to insinuate that
their prosecutors are informers, and prosecutors, in their anxiety
to prove they are not informers, sometimes go so far as to claim
to be personal enemies, or even hereditary enemies, of the accused.
Nevertheless, informers seem to have plied a busy trade, principally in blackmailing rich men who had guilty consciences or
disliked facing the ordeal of public trial. This state of affairs
naturally caused the propertied classes much anxiety, and perhaps
caused them to exaggerate the real scope of the evil.

Secondly, Athens, like all ancient States, lived from hand to
mouth, and reckoned on the penalties inflicted by the courts as a
regular source of income. It was therefore a temptation to jurors
to vote in the interests of the treasury when money was short,
and an informer dangled before their eyes a fat estate whose
owner, he alleged, had been guilty of some serious offence. In this
respect also Athens was not unique; Roman emperors short of
money are alleged to have encouraged *delatores* and made good
the finances by confiscation. Nor need one go so far afield as the
Roman empire for a parallel. The Athenian oligarchs in the Thirty
filled their treasury by condemning a number of innocuous but
wealthy citizens and metics to death and seizing their property.
This situation also made the propertied classes nervous, and probably made them exaggerate the evil. There is no reason to believe
that all large estates confiscated were confiscated because they
were large. Rich Athenians were quite capable of cheating the
treasury or betraying the interests of the State; and it is, for instance, very unlikely that a statesman of such severe probity as
Lycurgus would have secured the confiscation of the huge estate
—160 talents—of Diphilus, unless he had been guilty of a serious
breach of the mining laws.

There are three passages in Lysias which allude to the abuse.
In a speech written in 399 a litigant states that "the council for
the time being, when it has enough money for the administration, behaves correctly, but when it gets into difficulties it is
obliged to receive impeachments and confiscate the property of
the citizens and listen to the worst of the politicians." In another
speech, written about ten years later, another litigant says to the

jury: "You must remember that you have often heard them (his opponents) saying, when they wanted to ruin someone unjustly, that, if you would not condemn the people they tell you to condemn, your pay will fail. And in a third speech, delivered in 387, a man accused of detaining the confiscated estate of a relative complains: "My defence is difficult in view of the opinion some hold about Nicophemus' estate, and the present shortage of money in the city, my case being against the treasury." These are serious allegations, and indicate an unhealthy state of affairs. But it is to be noted that they all occur in the period following the fall of Athens, when the State was almost bankrupt, and when, despite the amnesty, feeling against the rich, many of whom had backed the Thirty, was very bitter among the mass of the citizens. I have not detected any other similar suggestion in all the later speeches, forensic or political, of the orators, except one sentence in the Fourth Philippic of Demosthenes, when, after appealing to the rich not to grudge to the poor their theoric payments, he turns to the poor, and says: "But where does the difficulty arise? What is the trouble? It is when they see some people transferring to private fortunes the practice established for public moneys, and a speaker is great in your eyes at the moment, and immortal as far as security goes—but the secret vote is different from the open applause. This breeds distrust and anger." This very guarded passage seems to mean that the rich suspected that the poor wished to increase their payments from public funds by confiscating private property, and that rich men who were applauded in the assembly were condemned by the secret ballot of the juries. Hypereides, a few years later, takes pride in the disinterested justice of Athenian juries:

"There is no people or king or nation in the world more magnanimous than the people of Athens. It does not abandon to their fate those of the citizens, whether individuals or classes, who are falsely accused, but goes to their rescue. In the first place when Teisis denounced the estate of Euthycrates, which was worth more than sixty talents, as being public property, and after that again promised to denounce the estate of Philip and Nausicles, alleging that they acquired their wealth from unregistered mines, the jury, so far from welcoming such a speech or coveting other men's goods, promptly disfranchised the false accuser, not giving him a fifth of the votes. And again does not the recent action of the jurors last month deserve great praise? When Lysander denounced the mine of Epicrates as having been sunk within the boundaries—the mine he had been working for three years and pretty well all the richest men in the city were his partners—and Lysander promised to bring in 300 talents for the city—that is what he said they had got out of the mine—nevertheless the jury paid no attention to the accuser's promise but looked only to justice and declared the mine private."

Hypereides perhaps protests too much, but he does at least provide concrete instances when Athenian juries resisted very tempting baits.

If one may attempt to draw a general conclusion it would be that informers were a nuisance to the rich at Athens, and that the Athenian courts were sometimes tempted, especially in financial crises, to increase the revenue by condemning rich defendants on insufficient evidence. Neither of these abuses was, however, peculiar to a democratic régime.

These are the main criticisms brought by the philosophers against the Athenian democracy. Some are directed against abuses which democrats agreed to be such, the overriding of the law by the executive enactments of the assembly and the spoliation of the rich by the poor, but which they claimed to be alien to the principles of democracy. In these matters the Athenian people was certainly not beyond reproach, but on the whole the charges seem to have been exaggerated, and the Athenians were probably justified in claiming that arbitrary violence of this kind was more characteristic of oligarchic régimes than of their own.

Other criticisms are on points of principle and are based on an entirely different conception of the functions of the State and an entirely different estimate of human nature. The philosophers held that the State ought to mould and train the citizens in virtue, and assumed that the average man was naturally evil or a least foolish. Political power must therefore be given to a select group of wise good men, who would impose a good way of life on the rest by a rigid system of education and control. The Athenian democrats, on the other hand, took an optimistic view of human nature, and believed that every citizen should be allowed to live his own life in his own way, within the broad limits laid down by the law, and that all citizens could be trusted to take their part in the government of the city, whether by voting and speaking in the assembly, judging in the juries, carrying on the routine administration as magistrates, or selecting the men to hold high political office. On one point the Athenians were distrustful of human nature, on its ability to resist the temptations of irresponsible power; hence their insistence on brief terms of office, regular review of the conduct of magistrates in office, and above all a searching scrutiny of the record of magistrates on completing their term. The philosophers are strangely blind to this danger, and are content to rely on the virtue of their usually hereditary or co-optative oligarchies of wise men.

The ideals of the Athenian democracy are perhaps best summed up in a rather florid passage of the Funeral Oration attributed to Lysias. Our ancestors, he says,

"were the first and only men of that time who cast out arbitrary power and established democracy, holding that the freedom of all was the greatest concord, and sharing with one another their hopes and perils they governed themselves with free hearts, honouring the good and chastising the bad by law. They held it bestial to constrain one another by force, and the part of men to define justice by law, and to persuade by reason, and serve both by action, having law as their king and reason as their teacher."

[Professor Jones concludes with a rather detailed analysis of Thucydides' criticism of Athenian imperialism, foreign policy, and conduct of the Peloponnesian War, summing up as follows:]

The Athenians, in fact, can only be condemned, if they are judged by much more lofty standards than were normally applied to international relations. Why did Thucydides take so uncharitable a view of his native city? His attitude was partly due to a misconception of public feeling natural to a man of his class, particularly when he had for many years lived in exile in oligarchic circles. He appears to have really believed that the Athenians were hated by their allies, whereas the Peloponnesian League was a free association of cities. But his attitude was also probably due to a deep-seated and perhaps unconscious desire to find a moral justification for the fall of Athens. It was not enough to say that it was due to the folly of the democratic politicians whom he so much disliked. It must have been deserved. Athens had suffered grievously; this could not have been so if she had not sinned greatly.

The opinions of Thucydides, Plato and Aristotle have naturally carried great weight, and so, curiously enough, have those of Isocrates. In the absence of any coherent statement of the democratic case, most modern historians have rather uncritically accepted the oligarchic view of Athens, and condemned what Aristotle calls the "extreme democracy." In this article I have endeavoured to reconstruct the theory of government in which democrats believed and to assess the merits and defects of the Athenian democracy in the conduct of home affairs and of foreign and imperial policy. My readers can judge whether the "extreme democracy," in which the people was sovereign, and vulgar persons who worked with their hands enjoyed full political rights, including access to all offices, and owing to their greater numbers preponderated in the assembly, was indeed so pernicious a form of government as Athenian philosophers and historians represent.

15   *Arnold Gomme: The Democracy in Operation*

The late Arnold Gomme (1886–1959) was a passionate defender of the things he loved, and two of the things he loved most passionately throughout a long and active life were political liberty and the Greek world. Professor of Greek at Glasgow University, Gomme was a man much admired by his colleagues and contemporaries, but not because of any gentle spirit of complacency or quiet unassuming manner. Gomme was devoted to setting people straight, and while crusading vigor might sometimes lead him to overstate a case, his scholarship, his style, and his flair for cutting right to the heart of a matter made him a formidable opponent and a compelling advocate. The following article is a typically energetic defense of the government of the common man in Athens.

The French historian Gustave Glotz said of the Athenians that they turned what should have been an organ of control into an organ of administrative action. The criticism explicit in this statement may well be just; but let us forget it, and substitute for "should have been" the words "has been normally in other democracies"; the Athenians turned what elsewhere has been an organ of control—the popular assembly, plebiscites or general elections in larger states—into an organ of administration, that is, of legislative and, more important, of executive action. How did they manage it? Not "Was this wise or foolish?" but "How did it work at all?" How can mass meetings—meetings which were not even given an experienced chairman—deal with legislative and executive problems?

Let us first make it quite clear that they were mass meetings, and that they did deal with these problems. Thousands attended them; and we know, from the keen-sighted and sympathetic wit of Aristophanes, from the equally keen-sighted but less sympathetic criticism of Plato, as well as from the testimony of Thucydides, that these thousands were drawn from all classes of men, artisans, peasants and shopkeepers, merchants and manufacturers, aristocrats and plebeians, rich and poor, the humble and the ambitious—all of them also at some time or other in their lives soldiers or sailors, a matter of moment in a democratic state that was often at war. Thucydides indeed, in a well-known passage, says that the oligarchs of 411 B.C. argued that not more than 5000 citizens (out of 30,000 or more) ever attended the assembly; but note the reasons they gave: . . . service in the army and activity overseas—

SOURCE. A. W. Gomme, "The Working of the Athenian Democracy," *History* 36, 1951, pp. 12–28. Reprinted in *More Essays in Greek History and Literature*, Oxford: Basil Blackwell, Publisher, 1962. Copyright 1951. Reprinted by permission of Basil Blackwell & Mott, Ltd.

in other words, they were thinking of the war conditions just of that time. In peace, or during the Archidamian war, conditions were different. (In passing, if I may digress, we may note that, by this argument, which is so lovingly followed by those historians who do not like the Athenian democracy, it was the younger men, the soldiers and sailors, the latter especially, who could not attend many of the meetings; why did not the older generation, whom the more simple-minded among us, the willing victims alike of the comedy of Aristophanes and the commonplaces of Isokrates, believe to have been wisely and consistently opposed to the war, why did they not take the opportunity to end it? But to return.) I do not deny that the use of much slave labour made political activity for all classes easier than it would otherwise have been; nor that those who lived in or near Athens itself attended more often than distant countrymen, and may have from time to time, though not during the Peloponnesian war, dominated it. But I do not believe in the picture of Athenian citizens as a leisure class supported by the tribute of subject cities. For one thing, the same type of democratic government was at work in the fourth century when there were no subject cities and no tribute; and for another, if all citizens were leisured, what becomes of Plato's criticism that men cannot do two things well—attend both to their own and to public affairs—and of Perikles' assertion that at Athens they could? Mass meetings therefore they were (even 5000 would make a mass meeting), and of all sorts of people, the majority of them workers and comparatively poor men.

Secondly, did this assembly really rule? or were its meetings only an empty show, and all decisions made elsewhere? We can make a simple test: when government is by discussion, as it certainly was in Athens, where did the discussion take place, where were the great speeches made? In this country, in the eighteenth and early nineteenth centuries, they were made in parliament, in the Lords or the Commons, with a growing preponderance of the Commons; in the later nineteenth century in the Commons and on the hustings; now over the radio as well; the House of Commons, with some control by the people, rules. In Rome, in the great days of the Republic, the speeches were made in the senate; for the senate ruled. In Athens they were made only in the assembly. (I believe that we have only one mention of speeches in the *boulê* or council, in Aristophanes, in that brilliant parody of a debate in the *Knights*.) Government, then, was by the people. The assembly, that is, ruled in fact: if we make a very rough comparison with modern practice we might say that, as the Athenian assembly chose the principal officers of state, so does the modern electorate choose, though in most countries indirectly, the government . . . secondly, that the assembly also controlled finance and legislation, that is, voted moneys and passed laws, which with us is the concern of parliament, and decided questions of foreign and domestic policy—war and peace, alliances (when ambassadors of foreign powers would appear before it), the nature and size of the armed forces—which are now decided by parliament and government combined; and thirdly, that this assembly had functions, for example in war-time the decision to send an army or a fleet on a particular campaign, its size and composition and its commanders, which are now the exclusive concern of the executive. Government *by* the people with a vengeance; and Thucydides is full witness to this. Contrast what can be said now—one of the difficulties of democratic government for us is the relation of the people, whose will *ex hypothesi* must prevail, to a parliament; and the more stable the form of government, the more powerful will be the parliament, and the greater its moral authority: *The Times* said not long ago in a leading article, "The problem which recurs in every age is that of the relation of delegate to principal. The people are the source of political authority, but cannot govern. They must commit the function to representatives; in Mr. Amery's succinct phrase, we have 'government of the people, for the people, with but not by the people'."

It is not sufficient to say that it was possible in a small community like the ancient Greek states, the largest of which had no more than 35,000–40,000 citizens, who all lived within 25 miles or so of the political centre and most very much nearer: and for two reasons. Firstly, even in these conditions the majority, busy with their own affairs, cannot meet very often—the very politically minded Athenians restricted themselves to forty meetings of the *ekklesia* a year, at least in the fourth century, and many of these must have been formal; and public business is a day-by-day affair.

Secondly, a mass meeting of thousands, even if no more than 5000, is not by itself a suitable organ—one might say, *by itself* not a possible organ—for the conduct of public affairs; and in fact not many Greek states whose affairs were as important as those of Athens did conduct them in this way. A small state, that is to say a Greek small state, was not necessarily a democracy of the Athenian type, with effective government by the people. And, in order that this Athenian type may work at all, two other things are essential: somebody—one or two words—somebody or some body—there must be to deal with affairs from day to day; and somebody to prepare business for the mass meeting, the *ekklesia*, or the meeting will accomplish nothing; it will go astray. Of these two activities the latter was, for the working of the democracy, the more important; to whom could it be entrusted? The Athenian solution of this problem, which was the institution of a council or *boulê* to perform both functions—day-to-day affairs and the preparation of business for the *ekklesia*—is really the theme of this paper.

Every state must have an executive of some kind—magistrates in the widest sense of the word—to which more or less wide powers are granted, on whom more or less effective checks can be imposed. Among the powers granted to the executive in some ancient states was that of preparing business for, and presiding over, meetings of the assembly of citizens: notably this was the case in Rome—the consuls for the important *comitia*, the tribunes for the *concilia plebis*—in the days, that is, when the assemblies counted for something. Now everyone knows how important these duties are, in any society, from a national parliament to a learned academy or private club. Give those duties, as Rome did, to men who are already powerful—powerful because they are popular in some way, popularly elected, because they are magistrates with specific authority, and above all because they are in the know—they know what is going on far better than the majority of their fellow-citizens—and it is seen at once what influence they will have at the assembly, the mass meeting, when in effect they decide what questions are to be put. The assembly will be, at best, an organ of control only.

Athens was not going to allow any such powers to her executive officers. None of them presided over or prepared business for her *ekklesia*, nor had any special functions in it, except that the most important, the *stratêgoi*,[1] could demand a special meeting of the *ekklesia* to deal with some urgent matter. Naturally, the executive often had matters to report to the *ekklesia*, and therefore were given first hearing; naturally also, if they had been elected to office because they were well known and popular, they would at any time be listened to and applauded; they would sway the meeting; but as citizens like any other, not by right as magistrates. And it is highly characteristic of Athens that many of her most influential politicians for long years held no office at all, and fought shy of it; they were content with their influence as talkers, and wanted no further responsibility. It is equally characteristic that the Athenians would have no permanent president of the *ekklesia*, only a chairman and a sort of chairman's committee for each meeting: a man chosen to preside at every meeting, even for a limited period, would have much too much power.

So these indispensable duties were given to a council, the *boulê* of 400 members instituted by Solon, changed to that of 500 by Kleisthenes, a sort of general purposes committee of the assembly. But Athens already had a council, the *Areiopagos*, a body much respected, even revered, which Solon certainly did not wish to push on one side, nor apparently Kleisthenes: yet it was not given the duty of preparing business for the assembly, as it might have been. The *Areiopagos* was, like the senate at Rome, recruited from the higher magistracy: a man who had been elected one of the nine annual *archons* became a member of it after his year of service, and, in the ordinary way, a member for life. Had Solon's constitution survived it might have become the all-important council of the city, for it would contain within it, as did the Roman senate, all the most important executive experience and would develop its own methods of influence because its members did not change. Give it the function of preparing the business of the assembly as well, and there would be scarcely any limit to its power. It was in Solon's day also an oligarchic body, because the *archons* were chosen from the richer classes; Solon wished to

[1] Ten annually elected generals, one from each tribe. *Ed.*

preserve this feature, but wanted a democratic check on them
too. For this he must free the assembly from the influence both
of the magistrates and of the *Areiopagos*; and the only way this
could be done was by giving it its own council as general purposes
committee. Without any committee, it would be ineffective, because it could not function in any orderly way; with a powerful
external body as its committee, it would have been weak because
it would have been controlled. Solon was truly regarded as the
father of the Athenian democracy: he had rescued the assembly,
saved it for democracy, so to speak. An assembly of some kind
was age-old and found in every Greek state, as in Rome: Solon
saw to it that in Athens it should be politically important, effective
—firstly, by freeing so many of its proper members from economic
slavery, so that the assembly was properly constituted, open to
all citizens; and secondly, by making it independent of all other
powers in the state by giving it its own general purposes committee. Aristotle, who noted so clearly the former as the essential
preliminary to democracy in Solon's reforms, did not notice the
importance of the latter; and modern scholars have sometimes
continued his neglect.

How important it was can be seen in the history of the century
or so after the overthrow of the tyrants in 510 B.C. One of Kleisthenes' first actions then, in establishing a democratic form of
government, was the restoration of this council in a new form as
the *boulê* of 500—not the restoration of the *ekklesia*, for that, in
theory at least, and however enfeebled, had always been there;
but he must make its authority effective. The first action of the
oligarchs in their revolution of 411 B.C. is to turn out the *boulê*,
and set up one of, practically, their own choice; they do indeed
try to introduce some modification in the membership of the
assembly as well, but it is the overthrow of the *boulê* which is the
necessary first step in establishing an oligarchy. And this procedure is exactly followed by the Thirty and the Spartan garrison
in 404: in form not the assembly, but the *boulê*, is suppressed. It
is the essential cog-wheel of the machine: without it the machine
will not work.

But what was to prevent this council itself from obtaining
power, if only gradually and unnoticed, at the expense of the

assembly? It was fully representative of the people—it had that sort of authority—and it had important duties. As a body or through a committee it met daily and did the day-to-day work of the state; it received ambassadors of foreign states; it worked with the *stratêgoi* and other executive officers; it had some executive powers of its own; and above all it prepared all the business of the assembly and gave a provisional opinion on all matters to come before it—the assembly put this restriction on itself, and on the whole faithfully observed it, that it should consider nothing that had not previously been considered by the council. Large enough powers: why did no big debate take place in the council on the question of what should be brought before the assembly, or what should be the council's own "provisional" recommendation? or why did it not, in practice if not in theory, make decisions, and leave the assembly to be at most but an ultimate organ of control? This danger was met in a characteristically logical way.

The power of a modern parliament rests largely on that corporate feeling which is created when a number of people work together for a considerable number of years in the same place and on the same matters. No matter what genuine differences of opinion and outlook may exist within it or what the personal rivalries, all are at the same time, in relation to all other citizens, privileged members of parliament. (Think of the touchiness of our own parliament with regard to its privileges—not any longer those *vis-à-vis* the crown, but those *vis-à-vis* the public which has elected it. Think of the late James Maxton, so lonely in his convictions, but liked for his character: how good a parliamentatian he was.) The members form one body; they have power; they are the people in the know; they are in fact rulers. Robert de Jouvenel, in his book *La République des Camerades*, said: *"Il y a moins de différence entre deux députés dont l'un est révolutionnaire et l'autre ne l'est pas, qu'entre deux révolutionnaires dont l'un est député et l'autre ne l'est pas"*:[2] an acute and penetrating observation which has perhaps in recent years lost a little of its truth by

---

[2] "There is less difference between two deputies of whom one is a revolutionary and the other is not, than between two revolutionaries of whom one is a deputy and the other is not."

the adoption of a new technique of revolution by the Communists, but which was certainly true up to ten years ago. It applies of course not only to parliament, but to other politically important bodies—central committees of parties, executives of the T.U.C. or C.G.T., and many others. The Roman senate was the best example of such a council in ancient history: consisting as it did in practice of ex-consuls, ex-praetors, etc., members for life, it contained within itself all the influence that comes from executive command, political experience, and from popularity itself whenever the people had exerted itself in the election of magistrates; its members all knew each other, they all had certain privileges, they were all in the know. Even without that conservative tendency of the Romans which led them continually to elect to office members of the senatorial families (so that the newly-elected and perhaps ambitious young consul and senator found himself met by the frowns and the equally formidable smiles of his father, his uncles and his cousins—his own set), such a council was bound to have real power, more power than any assembly of the ignorant, especially an assembly presided over and led by magistrates—no matter how clearly the constitution laid it down that only the assemblies could pass laws, make war and peace, and elect those magistrates who will later become members of the senate. The assembly at Athens also passed laws, made war and peace, and elected the magistrates; but there laws were debated, foreign ambassadors came before it to discuss war and peace or alliance, and there was no council that ruled. The *Areiopagos* had lost its influence when the lot was introduced in the election of the *archons* from which it was recruited; henceforth the politically able and ambitious did not become *archons*, and the *Areiopagos* lost all that authority which comes from being the home of experience, like the senate at Rome. The council of 500, the assembly's own council, never acquired such influence, because from the first, as though consciously to avoid such danger, the Athenians decided that election to the council was to be for a year only, that no one could be elected more than twice, and that (how they did think of everything)! not in successive years. (The lot was used in the election: but this I think was not in this case of primary importance; for

when such a large proportion of the citizens were to serve on the
council once at least in a lifetime, the lot was used rather to determine the order in which they should serve than to keep out the
ambitious and dominating. It was also of importance in bringing
on to the council citizens of small and outlying *demoi* who might
otherwise never have appeared in Athens.) This simple device—
not more than two years on the council for anyone and those
years not consecutive—prevented the growth of anything like that
corporate feeling which comes when men work side by side for
many years together, and which is so powerful a factor in the
creation of privilege; the councillors were strangers to each other,
at least as much as any other men in a small community, and we
must remember that Thucydides, contrasting Athens with much
smaller states, notes that the conspirators of 411 B.C. had an easier
task because in a large city men did not know one another. It
prevented also the concentration of political experience in a small
body of men, and at the same time spread political experience
among as large a number of citizens as possible; and in this way
worked both positively and negatively towards the predominance
of the assembly. For with service as councillor for never more
than two separated years, a citizen did not get so much more
experience, nor influence, than his fellows, important and indispensable as his work was; and with at least 250 becoming councillors for the first time every year and the same number retiring
into the citizen body for good (probably many more than 250
on the average, for there is no reason to suppose that the majority
of councillors did serve their two years), from a quarter to a third
or more of citizens over thirty at any one time had had such
political experience as membership of the council gave; the difference, that is, in experience and knowledge, between the average
councillor and the average citizen in the assembly at any time was
not great. Most of the citizens had had, as councillors and in one
of the many minor administrative offices, some close experience
of the day-to-day conduct of state affairs, none had had much.
Doubtless the ambitious and the intriguers got their names put
down as candidates for the council, and the humble and retiring
did not: Kleon and Demosthenes, typical *polypragmones*, busy-

bodies, were councillors, though perhaps not more than once; but Sokrates, the least ambitious of men, served too when the lot fell to him. So that Athens avoided the difficulty inherent in the large modern state, which was so well put in the maxim of de Jouvenel: she knew no long-lived body like a parliament or a party executive, or a permanent council like the Roman senate. She also had no skilled bureaucracy; but this I think is less important; it illustrates the much greater simplicity of public affairs in the small city state rather than anything else. It is the absence of a parliament which is important: both knowledge and experience of affairs were shared by a majority of the population. There was very little difference in Athens between two men of the same party one of whom was, for the moment, a deputy and the other was not.

We have therefore this apparent paradox: the council is so important that it is indispensable; it is the lynch-pin of the democracy; it is the first object of attack by the enemies of the democracy; but it is not powerful. By its activity, its effective execution of its many duties, it secured the predominance of the assembly and so its own subordination: government of the people, for the people, *and* by the people.

I should perhaps add that when I say "Athens avoided this difficulty" or "knowledge and experience were shared," I am speaking comparatively, not absolutely: this was much more nearly true of Athens than of any other important state—any other state, that is, that has been large in its own world, that fought wars against even larger states, that for a time ruled an empire, that had a large commerce and an imposing financial structure, that entered into alliances and was a member of a league of nations, that knew great victories in war and crushing defeat and survived both, that above all knew what orderly and free government meant and, by and large, did not abuse its powers. There were of course in Athens many simple, ignorant men (ignorant of politics, I mean), just as there were clever knowing ones, with sharp little eyes: men like the chorus in *Oedipus* (a strangely unaristocratic chorus, though they are addressed as chiefs of Thebes), who answer an awkward question of Kreon

with the words "I do not know: I do not see what the rulers do,"
or the conventional farmer of Euripides' *Orestes*, rough in appearance but brave, who seldom came to the city for public meetings,
for he had his own work to attend to, "but intelligent," and the
poor peasant of *The Suppliants* who, though no fool, yet was too
busy to be able to have an eye on public affairs; Demosthenes'
"innocent and quiet people," best shown in that excellent scene
in Aristophanes' *Peace* where, when Hermes has explained the
origin of the war in the misfortunes of Pheidias and Perikles' fear
of being implicated, first Trygaios says that he had never heard
that tale before, then the chorus add "Nor I, till now. A lot of
things happen above our heads. And these were not innocents,
but waspish *dicasts* whose temper Perikles had been afraid of.
We must bear all this in mind, especially when we read in the
funeral speech in Thucydides the proud claim that Athenians
were not prevented by private business from attending to the
city's affairs. But we are, as I said, speaking comparatively: compared with any other people who have played so important a part
in politics, it is true that de Jouvenel's maxim does not apply to
the Athenians, that they did enjoy, or suffer from, government by
the people.

And it was consciously intended; let us look at one detail. The
council of 500 was itself rather large for meeting *every* day: it was
divided into 10 "presiding committees" consisting each of them of
the 50 members of a *phylê*, and each of these groups of 50 served
in turn for a tenth of the year, actually sitting every day of its
turn, for the day-to-day business. The order in which they were
to serve was determined by lot; but, fearful lest undue influence
might be exerted or something "wangled" if it were known
beforehand in what order all the groups would serve in the course
of the year, lots were drawn at the end of each period to decide
which group should preside next, so that, except for the last
period, it was never known beforehand which group would form
the next committee. Further, neither the assembly, as I said above,
nor the council and its committees had a permanent chairman,
for that would give far too much power to the individual because
he would know the ropes: instead, the presiding committee of

the council elected by lot a new president every day (so that 36 or 37 of its 50 members would be chosen),[3] if a full meeting of the council was to be held the president of the committee for the day would preside; if the assembly was to meet, the same man would preside there with some others in support. (In the fourth century, as a refinement on this, because, I suppose, the choice was a little too narrow, another elected by lot from the councillors who did *not* form the presiding committee presided at the assembly.) No one was in the chair at these multitudinous and sometimes tumultuous assemblies more than once in his life. At these assemblies debate was free: the president announced the business, the "motion before the house," and the provisional vote of the council; and then asked, "who wishes to speak?"

I need not say much about popular control of the executive, of the officers of state, at Athens, because it is familiar. The "specialists"—so far as Athens listened to specialists at all—generals, engineers, architects, doctors—were elected by vote; the others by lot; all for a year only. (Election of specialists by popular vote would seem to us as absurd a method as the lot; but it must be admitted that the men who elected Pheidias and Iktinos, and who gave so many prizes to Sophokles, did not choose so badly.) By a fine stroke of logic the specialists could be re-elected any number of times, the rest only once in a life-time, so that again the chief purpose of the lot was to decide the order of service and to secure a fair distribution. All were subjected to an audit at the end of their year, or in the middle of it if the assembly so wished, before auditors themselves elected by lot and subjected to the same rules. When I said at the beginning of this paper that the great political speeches in Athens were made in the assembly, I was of course inaccurate, but not, I think, misleading: many of them were made in the law-courts when public men were on trial. So also in Rome; but in what very different law-courts! For the *dicasteries* at Athens were also mass meetings, especially in political trials, with 1000 or more jurors and no skilled judge

---

[3] There were ten of these "presiding committees"; so in a year of 365 days, half would serve for 36, half for 37 days. (At other times a lunar calendar was in use, with many resulting complexities.)

to guide them—they were judicial committees, as it were, of the assembly. I would like to mention two points. As I have already said, no elected, and therefore influential, because popular, magistrate held any office in the assembly itself; but besides this, note a particular contrast with early Rome. There a special office, the tribunate of the *plebs*, had been instituted for the protection of the individual citizens against oppression by the magistrates, especially the magistrates invested with *imperium*. . . . No such thing in Athens; no such office was necessary—instead "anyone might prosecute" a magistrate. Aristotle noted as the second of the specially democratic elements in Solon's constitution, this law that anyone might prosecute. And just as a meeting of the assembly began, after prayer and other formalities, with the president's question, "who wishes to speak?" so at the annual audit of magistrates the question was put, "who wishes to prosecute?"

The second point is this: in modern parliamentary states (I mean those in which the executive is dependent on a majority in parliament) if a government's policy is defeated in parliament, on a major issue, the government resigns, even though in other respects, as an administration, it may be approved. Necessarily so, because it is responsible for policy; it has the initiative (especially in this country if expenditure of money is involved, as it usually is); if it cannot command assent, its authority is so weakened that it could not carry on. But at Athens even so influential a man as Perikles, in so vital a question as war and peace, could find his advice ignored by the assembly, yet did not resign; for policy was not the business of the executive, but of the assembly, and any citizen in it could initiate it: Perikles often did, but because he was a persuasive speaker and a popular man, not because he held office as *stratêgos*. In the U.S.A. also Congress can ignore the President's policy and reject his advice, and he does not resign; but neither can Congress dismiss him from office nor diminish his powers, as a parliament can (in effect) dismiss a government which is part of it. The Athenian assembly could do both: dismiss him at any time, or ignore his advice and retain his services.

This remarkable constitution worked: it did not break down. It had many weaknesses, all of which were pointed out by Athenians themselves. But it is surprising how little we hear of packed meetings or snap votes, or of meetings postponed or broken up by an abuse of "bad omens." The constitution lasted 200 years, longer, by the way, than any modern democracy has lasted so far. Its peace was only once interrupted by attempted revolution within, in the dark days of a long war; at other times, after military defeat so decisive that an enemy garrison was installed and imposed the change. When the garrison was got rid of, with remarkable steadfastness and decision, the Athenians would restore their beloved democracy, practically unchanged—they did not despair and waver because the world was not perfect, nor cry out that the fourth republic must by all means be different from the third and then give up hope because it turned out to be so very like. They had an almost unique genius for democratic politics, which must have been widespread amongst all classes of the population, but which is perhaps illustrated best by the fact that the rich, both the old rich and the new, were prepared to take their share in it, and not only to play their part in the assembly and in high executive office, to obtain by demagogic arts the power which previously they had claimed by right of wealth and birth, but as holders, for brief periods, of one or other of the many dignified offices to which men were appointed by lot. We are not accustomed to associate *sophrosyne*, sobriety of conduct, with the Athenians, especially in their politics; we prefer to quote the assembly which voted that Kleon should go to Pylos, which laughed at his idle boasting and light-heartedly risked the safety of the state: an example surely of reckless folly, and not a unique one. We do right; for the Athenians did the same. But think of the self-discipline required to carry through that meeting at all, to vote the resolution, however foolish, in a constitutional manner, so that it was effective, and that without an experienced chairman. And think of the more normal meetings that passed elaborate financial measures like those of Kallias in the fifth century, or such decrees as the alliance with Chios in 384 B.C. which seems so strangely up to date—the preliminaries of an Aegean pact carefully phrased to show that it is no infringement of that covenant of United Nations which we call the Peace of Antalkidas; that Aegean pact itself, five years later, which was openly stated to be a defensive measure against the encroachments of Sparta, though the "covenant" still stands, and carefully guarded, in words, against any encroachments by Athens; the ticklish negotiations with the automatic, aggressive and vain dictator, Dionysios of Syracuse, ending with a treaty for all time, or with the more distant and more reasonable kings of Sidon or the Kimmerian Bosporos; the detailed treaty—two and a half closely printed pages in a modern text—with the small island of Keos, after some fighting there between two parties who became, inevitably, pro-Athenian and anti-Athenian and who are proclaimed as loyal democrats and treaty-breakers respectively; or with the same island on the export of ruddle.

But I would rather leave this day-to-day politics, and remember two longer-lasting enactments of this democracy, because they imposed some limitation on the assembly and in a most interesting way. The Athenians were aware—none more so—of the dangers of hasty legislation, not only because the new law might be a foolish one, but because it might, unnoticed, conflict with an existing law not expressly abrogated, and confusion would result. In the fourth century, therefore, a legislative commission was set up, the *nomothetai*, which, after the assembly had given a general assent, examined a proposed new law principally with a view to seeing if the way was clear for it. But what sort of a commission was this, and what sort of examination? A body of 500 or 1000, in fact a *legislative* committee of the *ekklesia*, and the examination was conducted like a trial, with counsel for and against the new law, and no skilled man to preside. The other institution I had in mind is the *graphê paranomon*, whereby a decree of the sovereign assembly could be indicted, by anyone, as unconstitutional. This has been compared by Goodwin with the power of the supreme court in the U.S.A. to declare unconstitutional, and so invalid, an act of Congress, on the initiative of some citizen. The comparison is a useful one; but what a contrast between the courts: the half-dozen eminent judges of America, the *dicastery* of 1000 or more in Athens! One of the best moments in Athenian history was in just such a case: after the foreign occupation and undemocratic rule of 317 to 307 B.C. had been ended by the "liberation" in 307 by the Macedonian commander, Demetrios, and the democracy restored, certain persons were in danger, notably Theophrastos,

Aristotle's successor at the Lyceum, no friend of the people, a foreigner, and certainly friendly with the enemy just driven out; to get rid of him the democrats got a decree passed by the assembly that there were to be no schools of philosophy, that is corporate bodies owning property, set up in the city without previous consent of the people in the assembly. This was indicted by a *graphê paranomon*; and was declared by the jury of 1000 to be unconstitutional because it conflicted with a law of Solon which guaranteed freedom of association; so Theophrastos, the foreigner, the "collaborator," remained. Another good moment was that a hundred years earlier, in 403, when another foreign garrison left, an oligarchy had been overthrown and the city liberated—genuinely liberated this time: the decrees of amnesty for past actions were so wisely framed:

"All legal decisions in civil cases and all arbitration rulings made before the overthrow of the democracy shall stand,"

to avoid an intolerable reopening of old disputes, and to preserve contracts,

"but all pending criminal charges from the same time to be dropped, and a complete amnesty proclaimed, and no one shall refer to them. A new code of laws is to be considered and, once approved by the assembly, published; no one is to be tried except by a law thus published, none by an unwritten law; no decree, whether of council or of the people is to have force against this published law, and no law is valid against an individual, but only against one and all."

I mention these two actions with some emphasis, because they show the Athenian respect for law, their *sophrosyne*, and, what is perhaps more important, their understanding of the quality of law—surprising in a people who never developed a science of jurisprudence—as well as their courage in maintaining freedom of thought. This is what I meant when I said earlier that the *demos* on the whole did not abuse its powers—I was thinking of internal administration only. Yet, so weak is human nature, so utterly fallible, that at the same time as that assertion of law and freedom in 306, men indulged in the most fulsome and servile flattery of the prince who had "liberated" them, and the great act of amnesty in 403 was soon followed by the worst crime in Athenian history, the execution of Sokrates.

A last point: one thing that is fascinating about the Athenians is their complete awareness of the weakness of their democracy: not only the almost inevitable weakness of any democracy, or any form of government by discussion, in external affairs, as in dealings with a formidable enemy like Philip of Macedon, but the special weaknesses as well of their own—as we see in Aristophanes and Demosthenes. But they would not give it up, nor reform it out of all recognition in the interests of efficiency. They liked it; it was their life, or their political life. It is not really sensible to take a good poet from a hungry garret and set him in a fine house, if at the same time you destroy his poetry; nor should a scientific mission to Central Africa spend so much time, money and energy in perfecting its means of self-defence against possible attacks by man and beast that it has none left for its scientific purpose. One must risk something: Plato would have sacrificed all freedom and variety on the altar of wisdom and virtue; the Athenians deliberately risked security for the sake of the freedom and variety of life and thought which they prized so highly. They succumbed to the attacks of Philip because he was a better statesman and a better general than anyone they could produce. True: but at least it was Athens which succumbed, not an altered city which, in a vain attempt at efficiency for the sake of security, had tried to imitate a system which was her mortal enemy.

16   W. G. Forrest: The Realities of Athenian Government

It is far too easy to apply the terminology of political science to the activity of ancient societies. In this selection, W. G. Forrest, a professor of Ancient History from Oxford University, demonstrates the fallacies inherent in applying clichés like "lower classes" and "urban proletariat" to Athens of the fifth century (clichés, incident-

ally, that have long since been given up by political scientists). Forrest concludes that the catastrophe of the Peloponnesian War cannot be blamed, as many have argued, on the excesses of democrats, or on the inability of a democracy to rule an empire.

At the festival of Dionysos in spring, 415 B.C., in the seventeenth year of the Peloponnesian War, four months after Athens had attacked and destroyed the small and comparatively innocent island of Melos, three months before a vast expedition was sent out to add Sicily to her empire. Euripides produced one of his starkest tragedies, the *Trojan Women*, a bitter study of the useless cruelty of war, destructive for the conquered and no less demoralising for the victor. Troy has fallen and its women, led by the aged queen Hekabe, wait for the Greeks' decisions on their fate: bit by bit the news is brought, Andromache, the wife of Hektor, falls to Pyrrhos, Kassandra, the virgin prophetess, has been chosen by the Commander-in-Chief, Agamemnon ("What luck to find oneself in a royal bed," says the simple-minded messenger), Andromache's infant son is to be thrown from the walls of Troy: and Hekabe herself, after sharing the agony of daughter-in-law, daughter and grandson, is led off to slavery while what is left of her city goes up in flames. The disaster is complete but the misery of it is not Euripides' only concern—in a prologue, the gods Athena and Poseidon have set it in a wider context:

"Mad is the man who sacks a city; whoever makes a desert of temples and tombs, the sanctuaries of the dead, has laid up destruction for himself in time to come." (*Trojan Women*).

The sack of Troy and the sufferings of the returning Greeks lay eight centuries in the past in 415 but no one could miss the parallel: by implication this was a condemnation alike of Athens' policy in

SOURCE. W. G. Forrest, *The Emergence of Greek Democracy*, Toronto & New York: McGraw-Hill Book Company, 1966, pp. 9–44. Copyright 1966 by W. G. Forrest. Used by permission of McGraw-Hill Book Company.

the past and of her ambitions for the future. Only a very confident audience can stomach meat as strong as this.

Three years later, at the same tragic festival, the same author presented his *Helena*, a melodramatic fantasy of great charm and beauty but of little merit as, indeed with no pretensions as a serious dramatic work and of no immediate relevance: Helen had not eloped with Paris, she had waited innocently in Egypt while her husband Menelaos fought for ten years before the walls of Troy to recover not her but a phantom, created by the gods in her image to help reduce the world's surplus population; and to Egypt Menelaos comes at last, dragging the phantom with him, just in time to save his real wife's virtue from the designs of a wicked Egyptian king. There is not much tragedy here; rather, a romantic fairy-tale, dreamed up out of hare-brained mythology and clever-clever contemporary philosophy. But the explanation of the change of tone is obvious enough.

The first expedition to Sicily had largely wasted the campaigning season of 415 but settled down at last to besiege the richest prize of all, the city of Syrakuse. There, however, a combination of ill-luck and incompetent generalship gradually lost the Athenians the initiative; the fleet found itself bottled up in the Syrakusan harbour, the army was virtually besieged on land and a huge reinforcing fleet which arrived early in the summer of 413 was only in time to share the destruction of those already there. Incredibly Athens had lost the better part of her navy and something like a third of her total military forces—in 412 Euripides' audience had no confidence left, they wanted to forget reality.

In politics as in the theatre the Athenian could not face responsibility; for the first time in over fifty years he was prepared, even anxious, to let others take decisions for him, prepared to abandon his democratic constitution and hand over power to an oligarchy. Not for long, it is true—within a year of March 412 Athenians were laughing at an Aristophanic parody of the *Helena* in his *Thesmophoriazusae*, and, within three months of the oligarchic *coup* in May 411 which put all authority in the hands of 400 men, the 400 were overthrown and the administration was made over to "those best able to serve the state with their bodies and their resources," in fact to a body of 9000. Even this more liberal régime had lasted only nine months or so when full democracy was restored. Yet for all this resilience, a resilience which prolonged the war for six years more, the Athens of 415 was gone, and when, in 404, a Spartan fleet sailed into the Peiraieus, it did no more than confirm what most Greeks, even most Athenians, already knew, that an extraordinary experiment in imperialism had failed.

It was impossible to separate this imperialism from the democracy which had fostered it and political morals were soon drawn. Sparta boasted that her oligarchic constitution had remained unchanged through ten generations; a stable oligarchy, then, was better than a fickle, reckless democracy. Athens' greatness had been built up in early democratic days, before the lowest class of citizen, the men who rowed her ships, had begun to make themselves felt in politics; democracy, then, was admirable so long as half the *demos*, the lower half, showed no interest in working it. Athens had still been successful even under full democracy so long as one man, the aristocrat Perikles, was there to control it; radical democracy, then, was tolerable if radical democracy meant no more than dictatorship by consent. These morals all had in common that they laid the blame for disaster firmly on the ordinary Athenian. They also had in common that they were drawn by men who were not themselves ordinary Athenians. They were partisan views, yet they have inspired most judgments passed on Athens since—and they are more or less totally false.

To the modern historian Athens between about 460 and 400 B.C. presents many puzzling contrasts and inconsistencies. For a considerable part of the period, 443 to 429, she was led by Perikles (born about 490, died 429), the man who for all his noble birth had helped in his early years (between 462 and 451) to complete the democratisation of the constitution; who had gone on to redefine the basis of the great alliance that Athens had formed and led against the Persians (between 478 and 449) in such a way that it became virtually an Athenian Empire; who had so prepared Athens' resources, economic and military, that by 431 no other power or collection of powers in Greece could think of challenging her at sea or force her to fight on land; who, finally, had a vision of Athens and her role in the Greek world which, as presented by Thucydides in the Funeral Speech has worried schoolboys, excited their masters and enthralled idealistic historians ever since.

Perikles apart, these were also the years which saw the production of the last and greatest tragedies of Aeschylos, which covered most of the working life of the other great dramatists, Sophokles and Euripides, and of the comedian Aristophanes. Peace with Persia in 449 opened the way for the construction of a vast range of public buildings, sacred and profane, which included the Parthenon, the Hephaistion, the Odeion, stoas in the Agora, temples at Sounion and Rhamnous, and, a little later, the Erechtheion; some of the finest achievements of Greek architecture; alongside the architects, Iktinos, Mnesikles and Kallikrates, worked Pheidias and other sculptors, representing for example on the Parthenon frieze, that "union of common aims and individual freedom . . . an order which never breaks down though constantly looking as if it would" which is "a perfect illustration of the ideal of democracy . . . expressed in the funeral speech of Perikles" (Sir John Beazley).

This same Athens attracted to itself foreigners of genius, Herodotos of Halikarnassos, the inventor of history, philosophers like Protagoras of Abdera and Anaxagoras of Klazomenai, and they in turn inspired native Athenians to outdo them; Thucydides, whose narrative of the Peloponnesian War is one of the most penetrating pieces of political analysis ever written and, at the same time, a story full of compassion told with genius; and Sokrates, who turned philosophy, or at least one philosopher, Plato, for the first time towards the problems that have exercised it ever since.

In these fifty years, then, lies the essence of "the Glory that was Greece." But they were not all glory. The astonishing intellectual and artistic achievement is over-shadowed from time to time by vicious attacks on its finest products: Aristophanes was impeached; Pheidias, Anaxagoras and Thucydides all went into exile; Sokrates was condemned to death and executed. The building programme was at least in part made possible by tribute exacted from the member states of the Empire; the continued subjection of this Empire was an integral part of Perikles' vision of Athens' greatness. Worst of all, Perikles' policies led directly to war with Sparta and the other leading powers of mainland

Greece in 431, a war which, for all his preparations, Athens lost, and which destroyed the vision utterly and beyond hope of recall.

There is nothing historians find it more difficult to forgive than failure. But an easy and comforting answer has lain ready to hand. Given those judgments passed on the Athenian *demos* by upperclass contemporaries or near contemporaries, like Thucydides or Plato, it was simple to find a scape-goat who was undoubtedly guilty at all times of some and sometimes of all the errors and crimes that had to be explained, a man, that is, whose faults were already writ large in the ancient evidence and could be condemned without any sense of personal guilt (modern historians too have not been men of the lower-class)—the ordinary Athenian.

The Athenian Constitution

Guilty indeed he must have been. No constitution has ever given more weight to the decisions of the ordinary man than did the Athenian. This constitution was a direct democracy, in which policy, even in matters of detail, was decided by an assembly of all adult male citizens; executive officers were appointed either by lot or by vote and their performance in office was carefully vetted by this same assembly. It met at a minimum forty times a year and as often besides as the chief executives thought fit. Proposals were introduced only by these executives or by members of the Council, but the assembly had full powers of debate, of amendment from the floor, and could even at times instruct the Council to introduce some specific proposal at a future meeting.

The Council itself, which was primarily responsible for formulating the Assembly's business and for a considerable part of the routine day-to-day administration, consisted of 500 members, chosen annually by lot from all parts of Attika, fifty from each of ten local tribes. No doubt many Athenians were unwilling to serve, no doubt anyone interested in politics could always get himself chosen, but no one acted as Councillor more than twice in his lifetime and the whole body must have been fairly representative of the citizen population, both economically and geo-

graphically. Then ten groups of tribal nominees took it in turn
to act as standing committee for the Council, a committee which
was in permanent session, living in the Council buildings, during
its period of office, while a daily chairman, again chosen at random
from the group, acted as president of the committee, Council or
assembly as and when each was convened.

It is, of course, notoriously difficult to draw a firm line between
administrative and policy-making decisions. In Athens, the chief
magistrates, the board of ten *strategoi* (or generals), the only important board filled by direct election, must always have influ-
enced and from time to time directed Athenian policy, even at
the highest level, as a result both of the nature of their office, since
military commanders must be allowed some freedom of decision,
and of their personal prestige, since their election in the first place
demanded considerable popularity. It was as *strategos*, regularly
reelected, that Perikles controlled the assembly during his supremacy. But, the *strategoi* apart (and even they were chosen,
directed and judged on their performance by the assembly), no
single Athenian or group of Athenians which was not a typical
and more or less random cross-section of the whole community
had a right to any significant say in the ordering of affairs without
the assembly's approval. The only body which might have put
a check on the assembly's independence, the Council, was itself
an assembly in miniature, moved no doubt to act against it from
time to time as a result of fuller information or more careful
thought, but never by a basic difference of interest.

Similarly, decisions in the law-courts, decisions which might on
occasion have momentous political implications, were reached by
juries of as many as 500 or 1000 men who were again drawn
indiscriminately from all who cared to present themselves for service. The professional speech-writer might have some effect on the
vote through the quality of the arguments he produced for his
client, but the presiding magistrate, the archon, who in any case
owed his appointment to lot, not to any judicial expertise, had
none at all. In origin the courts were committees of the assembly
or the assembly itself sitting in a judicial capacity to hear appeals
against a magistrate's personal judgment in a court of first instance,
and when, in time, the court of first instance and the appeal court

were, so to speak, combined, the archon brought with him to the
new proceedings nothing of his earlier authority. Throughout
their history the Athenian courts retained the essential characteristic that their judgments were amateur judgments which would
probably have been confirmed by any poll of the whole citizen
body.

Athenian Society: The "Demos." Thus Athens was run by
ordinary Athenians. But who were these ordinary Athenians?
When, where, and how did they go wrong? What were they
guilty of? The answers have taken many different forms; some
argue for a gradual degeneration of the *demos*, corrupted by
power; others that its naturally gross appetites, held in check
by Perikles, were let loose by his less scrupulous and less able,
because less well-bred, successors; others other things. But all
have in common that they distinguish sharply between the educated or "respectable" few and the selfish mob, or between the
squalid world of politics dominated by that greedy mob and the
secluded world of the intellectual which Perikles, in some mys-
terious way, is made to share. That is to say that the ordinary
Athenian becomes not an average Athenian, but something lower
and much nastier, and his responsibility is limited to political
decisions—and to the bad ones at that.

"The demagogues who thought themselves qualified to take
Perikles' place merely revealed the incapacity of a radical democracy to conduct a great war." (C. Hignett)

". . . the lower class which manned the fleet claimed the decisive
voice in affairs and swept the state onwards [sc. to defeat]."
(N. G. L. Hammond)

"Flattery had now become the means of government with respect to that plebeian mass . . . whose demands already give a
foretaste of the 'panem et circenses' of the Roman populace."
(A. Bonnard)

These are typical judgments. The "radical democracy," the
"lower class," the "plebeian mass" can be distinguished from
something less radical, less low, less plebeian. And who formed
the lower class?

"Athenians may conveniently be divided into oligarchs, moderates and radicals . . . roughly equivalent to the rich, the rural population and the urban proletariat . . . a classification also reflected in the military organisation . . . for the rich served as cavalry, the freehold farmers as the hoplites [the heavy-armed infantry] and the *thetes* [those who could not afford to provide themselves with armour] as marines or rowers in the fleet." (C. Hignett)

Now technically there is some truth in this. Since the days of Solon (594 B.C.) Athenians had been divided into four census classes, the *pentakosiomedimnoi*, men whose estates could produce 500 measures of grain or their equivalent per annum; the *hippeis* or cavalrymen, those who could afford to keep a horse and equip themselves for cavalry service; the *zeugitai* or hoplites, those fitted to arm themselves as infantrymen; and the *thetes*, those who could not. At first, as we shall see, these classes had an important political significance in that membership carried with it qualification for certain offices of state. In the fifth century this was still officially the case, at least to the extent that *thetes* were barred by law from the highest purely civil office, the archonship, and only *pentakosiomedimnoi* were trusted with the chief financial posts. But even with the archonship it seems unlikely that the law was strictly enforced and, although lack of military experience, not to mention lack of armour, would effectively keep *thetes* out of the *strategia*, all other offices, as far as we know, were open to them if they wanted them.

It is conceivable, then, even likely, that when military questions were to the fore men cared to what class they belonged and behaved according to the military interests of their class. It would be natural too if some snob value was attached to membership of the higher groups. But snobbery by itself does not create political parties and the classes can only be identified with political groupings if it can be shown either that military questions were always uppermost in Athenian minds (which they were not) or that the classes also corresponded with some other real economic, social or political distinction in the citizen body. The definition quoted above assumes that they do; *thetes* are an "urban proletariat," hoplites are freehold farmers, and, if this is right, such economic separation might certainly lead to political clashes.

But is it right? Nothing is easier for us than to imagine an industrial proletariat and to contrast it with what has almost become the modern historian's substitute for the noble savage—a sturdy peasantry tilling its sweet-smelling fields when out of armour. And, of course, there were many peasants in fifth-century Attika, some sturdy no doubt; there were also townsmen, though rather fewer in number. But the men who make up the urban proletariat known to us simply did not exist. Such factories as there were were manned by slaves, not by free labourers; there was not a single major job, domestic, industrial or agricultural, now performed by hired men which was not almost exclusively performed by slaves. The average Athenian was an independent property-owner, in the city an artisan, a trader, a shopkeeper or a manufacturer, in the country-town or village, an artisan, a shopkeeper or, more often, a farmer. Some were poor and worked alone; some were better off and employed a slave or slaves; almost all were independent. Nor is there any evidence to suggest, and it is indeed extremely unlikely, that there was any marked difference in the income range covered by the majority of the urban and the rural population. In short, there were hoplites in the town, *thetes* tilled the fields and, when the interests of town and country clashed, the political quarrel which resulted would divide *thetes* from *thetes*, hoplites from hoplites.

We can go further. A poor farmer or artisan today may see himself as something distinct from the successful farmer or artisan, may prefer to regard himself as a member of the "working class." But in a society where no working-class in our sense existed, how could he separate himself? What would he attach himself to? Where, in fact, could a meaningful line be drawn in the ascending scale of prosperity? And if one were drawn, which I doubt, why should it be precisely or even roughly at the point which separated *thetes* from hoplites?

Athenian society, then, was much more homogeneous than our own. Distinctions existed, between noble and commoner, between rich and poor, between hoplites and *thetes*, between countryman and town-dweller and these distinctions mattered from time to

time in politics as issues affecting different groups arose, but we
have no reason whatsoever for assuming that any one permanent
political group was defined by any one or any combination of
these distinctions. We see the typical Athenian often enough in
comedy or in the pages of the orators. He is by no means rich but
he is not a pauper: the chorus of Aristophanes' *Acharnians*, elderly
countrymen, charcoal-burners, hoplites and violently pro-war;
Dikaiopolis in the same play, a countryman again and probably a
hoplite, with at least one slave, but anti-war and thoroughly fed-
up with all politics and politicians; the chorus of the *Wasps*, townsmen probably, passionate democrats to a man, in their recollections
of the past sometimes hoplites, sometimes *thetes*; the poor hoplites
in a speech of Lysias who cannot afford their fare to Athens from
an outlying part of Attika to attend the hoplite muster and their
richer hoplite neighbour Mantitheos who generally provides it
(Speech XVI, sect. 14). These men cannot be broken up into any
neat and tidy classes.

But two other arguments have been used to suggest that the
politically effective *demos* was not typical of the whole *demos*,
that political decisions at Athens might tend to follow a lower
sectional, rather than the national, interest.

First it is argued that those who lived in the farther parts of
Attika would play a much smaller part in political life than those
who lived in and around the city. They would take their turn, if
they wished, on the Council but, when attendance at the assembly
or in the courts might mean a journey of a dozen miles or more,
few would feel inclined to make the effort except when their own
vital interests were affected. This is certainly true, but it becomes
important only if we once more admit ideas of an idle urban mob
or, still worse, allow the modern conurbation of Athens and its
port, Peiraieus, so to distort our picture of the ancient city that
the mob becomes tainted with the smell and interests of the docks
so that we find ourselves talking of "trading interests" or, yet again,
of the *thetes*, "the men who manned the fleet."

But the urban mob did not exist and the men who manned the
fleet did not live exclusively or even predominantly near the harbour. As for the traders, if they were not at sea and if they happened to be Athenian citizens (a substantial proportion of the

trading community was foreign), they could indeed attend to public business—if they were prepared for a five-mile walk. For the Peiraieus was as far from the assembly-place on the Pnyx in Athens as half-a-dozen substantial agricultural villages.

Indeed let us get the physical facts straight. Attika was some forty miles long from north-west to south-east and at its broadest some twenty-five miles wide; estimates of its total population in the fifth century vary considerably while even the real population must have fluctuated a great deal with the extraordinary expansion before 431 and the disastrous casualties of war thereafter, but it is very unlikely that it exceeded 80,000 at any point (the figures here and in what follows are for adult male citizens). The city walls of Athens itself enclosed an area rather less than one square mile; from them ran other walls to secure communication with the sea and especially with the Peiraieus, again an area of about one square mile; but outside these obvious centres there were many other significant settlements, at Eleusis, for example, and Acharnai, which, so Thucydides says, could furnish no less than 3000 hoplites, and elsewhere. Thucydides' figure must be exaggerated, but even if we halve it, even if we go on to believe that Archarnai was still by far the largest settlement outside Athens and, finally, assume that the "urban" population spilled over well outside the city walls, it is not easy to believe that this "urban" population numbered more than about 20,000 at the outside. Even if every one of these was of the lowest class (an absurd assumption) this is not a very impressive "urban proletariat" nor a very effective one, outnumbered as it would be three to one by countrymen none of whom could have lived more than twenty-five miles from Athens and of whom perhaps half were within about ten miles. Ten miles is not far to walk when a vital issue is at stake. Indeed during the Peloponnesian War, when most of the worst decisions are supposed to have been taken, a large part of the rural population sheltered from Spartan invasion behind the city walls—did not attend the assembly even then?

No, in war or peace there would be many small farmers queuing for their place on the Pnyx or in the law-courts hard on the heels of the city artisan and well in advance of the most energetic trader, and, given enough feeling, the rural vote could easily equal or exceed anything that the city could produce. In short the city did have a clear advantage in any normal circumstances; similarly the farmer from distant Marathon, the miner from Laurion, the fisherman or sailor of the east coast would be poorly represented, but there were other farmers, fishermen and sailors close enough at hand and the city itself was small enough to ensure that the geographical factor played no decisive part in determining the class-colour of Athenian political life.

Nor would the second factor which is often introduced—the existence of state-pay for public service in the magistracies, the Council and the courts. In theory this was designed to ensure that no Athenian should be barred by poverty from playing his part in public life. In practice, it is suggested, the prospect of financial reward for a day of idleness in the courts would attract the poorest among the citizens, the worst, the lowest, the laziest and most irresponsible. But even if we admit that the poor are bad, low, lazy and irresponsible, it is still not clear that they would be the most readily attracted. For one thing the pay was not substantial, for jury service little more than a bare subsistence wage, welcome perhaps to the destitute, such few as there were, but not markedly so to anyone who could survive on the fruits of his labour, and surely less attractive to those who depended entirely on their own labour than to their slightly wealthier neighbours. If the one abandoned his stall or his vegetable patch for a day his customers would go elsewhere, the weeds grow higher; a richer man could leave a slave behind to hold his scales or his hoe and have a happy evening on his juror's fee before going home.

Besides, we must set against the temptation of gain (and, of course, it is tempting) a lack of interest in and aptitude for affairs. The Athenians were probably more alive politically than any people has been since but it would still be strange if the normal pattern of political interest did not roughly repeat itself there. For one thing, not everyone cares about politics and even fewer care enough or in the right way to take action about them, particularly when things are going well and when there are no fundamental political issues in the air (and there were none in Athens between 462 and 411). For another, action takes time and not everyone has the time to spare, not only the time spent in office but the far greater amount that must be devoted to all the other (unpaid) activities that a politician, even a humble politician must attend to. This is clear enough at the highest level; all Athens' leading politicians were rich men, not only because there still survived some old aristocratic prejudice, but because only the rich could afford to devote themselves entirely to the political game. *Mutatis mutandis* the same was no doubt true at every level. It would be absurd to argue that the existence of pay made no difference, but I doubt whether it did more than make the office-holders of Athens slightly more representative than they would otherwise have been of the population as a whole. It certainly did not admit a flood of the impoverished to positions of importance. Indeed, in advancing this argument, the modern historian simply echoes another error of the contemporary critics of democracy—the idea that personal profit was the only attraction the régime had to offer to the ordinary man—and he will often cite one of these critics, Aristophanes, to support him. In his *Wasps* of 422 B.C. Aristophanes sets on the stage a chorus of jurymen who do indeed make much of the lure of the few shillings that their jury service provided. But Aristophanes *was* a critic (who would guess from right-wing comment to-day that working men ever work hard or like their job?), but fortunately a critic with far too much honesty and sympathy to be able to hide the fact that for all their verbal greed these laughable old characters fought for their places on the bench largely for the sheer pleasure of the job. A farcical comedy is not the place to emphasise a sense of civic responsibility but everything comic which goes with such a sense of responsibility is there—the love of power, the self-importance, above all the pride of the little man who finds himself able to face and frighten the big. If we stop to picture the real men behind the caricature they are our own town-councillors, school-governors, trade-union officials, even jurymen, not ne'er-do-well scroungers who think of nothing but turning an idle penny.

To return to the point. The Athenian political system favoured those who lived in or near the city; it may have encouraged some who would not otherwise have engaged in politics to take an interest, but the "plebeian mass," the greedy idle mob are still in fact the majority of the Athenian population, spread out among the poor and the comfortable, most of them independent, though very small, property- or business-owners, some oarsmen, some infantrymen, some countrymen, some townsmen, some old some young, some conservative some radical. Altogether a much less plausible subject for sentences which go on to ascribe to them one single aim, profit without effort at the expense of Athens' welfare as a whole. They themselves made up the whole.

Athenian Society: The "Elite." The intellectual or respectable are no less of a mirage. They existed, of course, but not in any ivory tower. Athens was too small, far too small, and Athenian society still too near the days of aristocratic versatility to admit the existence of two cultures, of such specialisation. Aeschylos was first and foremost a tragedian, but his tragedies turn time and again to the moral issues raised by contemporary politics, sometimes directly to politics themselves. Sophokles, the most accomplished of the tragedians, was one of Athens' chief financial officers in 443–442, served as a general in 440–439 and was called in as a senior constitutional adviser in 411. Even Euripides, a man who was regarded as a recluse in his own day, was not above writing two violently patriotic propaganda plays in the early days of the Peloponnesian War. Like Sophokles, the historian Thucydides served as a general and was exiled for his incompetence in the job. Even Sokrates fought in Athens' wars and held public office.

There is no doubt that the ordinary Athenian could be cruel, but nothing in the whole history of Athenian democracy could equal the cruelty, the blind monstrous stupidity of the few months in 411 and again in 404 when power was seized by the oligarchs, men whose leaders, almost to a man, were the favoured pupils and intimate friends of the "enlightened" philosophers; and Kritias, the worst of them all, had been loved by Sokrates.

The Athenian Achievement. The distinction, then, is false. The élite was not untainted by the sordid world of politics, the mob was not a mob. Throughout the period with which we are concerned upper-class Athenians, some cultivated, some not, devised and executed Athenian policy, which was sometimes wise, sometimes foolish, sometimes noble and sometimes wicked; throughout this same period the policies proposed were debated, accepted, modified or rejected by the mass of ordinary Athenians. They were not geniuses, they could at times be very stupid and very narrow-minded, but they were the men who listened to, voted for and presumably in some measure understood the "lofty idealism" of a Periklean speech; who commissioned temples from Iktinos and statues from Pheidias; who gave the first prize in tragedy to Aeschylos and Sophokles and, with admirable discretion, the second so often to Euripides.

In short, whatever our judgment on fifth-century Athens may be, it must be delivered on all Athenians. There is no trace of any coherent protest against what was obviously bad on the part of any one enlightened group; there is no trace of consistent opposition to what was good by the mass of ordinary men. All Athenians shared the optimism, the enthusiasm, curiosity, sense of adventure and love of experiment which characterises the artists and thinkers of the time; all Athenians were responsible for the development of the constitution in which they flourished and for the administration of the city from which they got their livelihood and their inspiration. All Athenians together committed one unforgiveable crime—they lost the Peloponnesian War.

Yet even this is not perhaps so serious as it seems now or seemed at the time. Like many other successful peoples, before and since, the Athenians had tried to do too much and failed, failed to make themselves masters of the whole of Greece, failed to export their democratic ideal as widely as some, including Perikles, had hoped. But it is worth remembering that for all their ambition they did not start the war which ruined them. That was Sparta's doing.

In 433 B.C. Athens had answered an appeal from an important naval power off the west coast of Greece, the island of Kerkyra, then threatened with attack by Sparta's most powerful ally in the Peloponnese, Kerkyra's own mother-city, Korinth. Korinthian pressure, working on the jealousy that Sparta had felt ever since Athens had taken over leadership of the anti-Persian alliance in 478 and on the fear that Athens was gradually overtaking her in power, influence and reputation as the leading state in Greece, soon persuaded even the less belligerent of the Spartans that war was justifiable and in 431 a Peloponnesian army under Spartan command crossed the Athenian frontier. As even the Spartans later admitted there could be no legal justification for this aggression. Not everyone would agree that they had absolutely no moral justification—would it have been right for the United States to attack Russia over Cuba or for Russia to bomb the States if, say, Rumania applied for membership of NATO? But it is at least certain that the vital decision, to make or not to make an alliance with Kerkyra, was not of Athens' seeking, and, once it had been thrust upon her, that she had virtually no alternative but to choose alliance. Given an awareness of Peloponnesian hostility (Sparta and her allies had come near to attacking her a few years earlier with even less reason on their side) she simply could not afford to let the large but hitherto neutral Kerkyran fleet be absorbed by Korinth. Perikles and the Athenian *demos* did not deliberately provoke the Peloponnesian War.

It is also worth remembering that along side Athens' one dramatic failure must be set a solid record of achievement, not only the intellectual achievement mentioned above but the superficially less spectacular though in fact even more impressive political achievement. Democracy took a nasty knock in 404 but, after a brief period of oligarchy at the moment of Sparta's victory, democracy was re-established, and re-established with extraordinary calmness, moderation and good sense. It survived for another eighty years and during that period it provided, as it had since 462, peaceful, moderate, efficient and popular government for the largest and most complex state in Greece.

For fifty years it had also administered an Empire which included almost all the Greek cities of the Aegean and its coasts, of the Hellespont and Propontis, and along the southern coast of Asia Minor as far as the Gulf of Antalya; in all some three hundred states, a few of them, Chios, Lesbos and Aigina for example, not much smaller than Athens herself when the alliance was first formed. This Empire is often described as a savage and selfish tyranny. A tyranny it certainly was, if by tyranny we mean no more than the domination of one state by another. But, although Athenian enthusiasm may have led her occasionally to impose or at least encourage democracy when it was not wholly necessary and although at times she might pursue her own economic advantage at the allies' expense, interference in their internal affairs, political, military, judicial and economic was in general no more than was needed for an efficient ordering of the whole—nominally, and to a considerable extent in fact, the ally remained autonomous.

Savageness and selfishness are even less justifiable charges. There were cases of brutality, oppression and extortion but they were few and, while personal profit was undoubtedly one of the chief motives that prompted Athens to maintain her hold, it was not the only one nor was the profit excessive. The tribute which helped her to build her temples and maintain her fleet was no great price to pay for the external security against pirates and Persians which she guaranteed; at its wartime peak, nearly three times higher than it was in 431, the total was probably something less than could be raised by a 5 per cent tax on goods entering and leaving harbours with which tribute was then replaced; little enough when we remember that payment absolved the allies from the responsibility of maintaining a fleet on their own account.

If Athenian rule was as harsh and unpopular as it seemed to the deliberately "realistic" Thucydides, it is curious how few of Athens' "subjects" were anxious to exchange it for Spartan free-dom—most of the allied contingents in Sicily preferred to face almost certain death beside the Athenians than to accept an offer of safety from the Syrakusans; curious that when revolts occur-red they were nearly always the work of dissident oligarchs while the people were often prepared actively to support the return of the Athenians; even more curious how many former members of the Empire were ready to join a new Athenian Confederacy in the fourth century after less than thirty years' experience of Spartan freedom.

That any outside rule should be thus tolerated, not to say wel-comed, shows that it was on the whole light, benevolent, profit-able and efficient and nothing could better illustrate the kind of service Athens could provide, the attention she was prepared to give, or remind us more vividly that all this was not the work of some high bureaucracy far removed from the day-to-day life of the mass of Athenians, than a series of decrees, passed in the early years of the war for the small city of Methone on the coast of the Thermaic Gulf. Methone had suffered some hardship and had failed to pay her tribute; she was also being harassed by her powerful neighbour, Macedon under its shifty king Perdikkas. The Athenians resolved [that] (I summarise):

The assembly should decide to reassess Methone's tribute or to be satisfied with a token payment.

If Methone stayed loyal it should receive special treatment with regard to the arrears of tribute.

An embassy be sent to ask Perdikkas not to interfere with Methone's trade or to march through her territory without permission.

If the embassy fail to produce agreement, both parties should send envoys to Athens for further discussions.

Methone should be allowed to import a certain amount of grain directly from the Black Sea and that the Athenian officials at the Hellespont should see to its safe passage.

Methone should be exempt from any general Athenian decrees about the Empire unless mentioned specifically in them.

A footnote adds that on the first point the *demos* decided to accept a token payment.

One small example of the kind of problem, trivial or vital, which engaged Athenian attention forty times a year; the answers added up to a record that was good both at home and abroad and the man responsible for them was an ordinary man. Whatever his failures or his failings, he demonstrated for the first time in human history that ordinary men were capable of government, that democracy was not, as some contemporary critics said, an "acknowledged folly."